The Nature Guide to
NEW ZEALAND NATIVE ORCHIDS

The Nature Guide to
NEW ZEALAND NATIVE ORCHIDS
Ian St George

Acknowledgements

I thank Dan Hatch and Bruce Irwin, not only for allowing me to use and modify parts of our jointly authored *Field Guide*, but for their unflagging enthusiasm and support for my efforts to advance the appreciation of New Zealand orchids. I thank Bob Bates (RB), Gillian Crowcroft (GC), Gael Donaghy (GD), George Fuller (GF), Dan Hatch (EDH), Bob Lamberts (R. Lamberts), Rob Lucas (RL), David McConachie (DM), Val Smith (VS) and Bob Talbot (RT) for the use of their photographs, and especially Vonnie Cave (YC) and Eric Scanlen (ES), whose artistry with the camera has enhanced this book greatly. I thank Peter de Lange for his careful criticism of an early draft. I am grateful to them and to the many members of the New Zealand Native Orchid Group who have reported where they have seen orchids and have thus helped in the compilation of the distribution maps; I have enjoyed their companionship on forays into the field, and their hospitality and humour on many memorable occasions.

A GODWIT BOOK
published by
Random House New Zealand
18 Poland Road, Glenfield, Auckland, New Zealand
First published 1999

© 1999 text: Ian St George; photographs: as credited

The moral rights of the author have been asserted

ISBN 1 86962 040 2

Cover illustration: *Thelymitra circumsepta* (RT)
Opposite title page: *Thelymitra pulchella* (IStG); page 6: *Thelymitra* 'Comet'
Printed in China

CONTENTS

INTRODUCTION   7
   Orchidomania   7
   Collectors   9
   Artists   11
   What is special about New Zealand orchids?   18
   Orchid habitatas   19
   Life cycle   20
   Flowers   23
   Pollination   25
   Fungi   28
   Names   32
   Maori and orchids   33
   The maps   35

NEW ZEALAND NATIVE ORCHIDS A–Z   37

A list of the New Zealand orchids   162
Table of flowering times   167
Derivations of specific names   170
Derivations of generic names   171
Reading list   172
Index   175

INTRODUCTION

Orchidomania

Why are orchid-fanciers so obsessed? What is the malady that a nineteenth-century writer called 'Orchid-o-Mania, which now pervades all (especially the Upper) classes'?

Even as he wrote, macho explorers were trampling the tropical jungles of the world searching out new plants for wealthy collectors. Many suffered; some lost their lives (explorers and orchids alike). Forests were deliberately burned to enhance the rarity of newly discovered plants. The orchid bestowed status, provided a sense of opulence, and fulfilled the Victorian craving for the bizarre. Why?

The question is worth asking, for the yearning goes on today. Meet an orchid enthusiast and you meet a person possessed. Is it the obvious, the extraordinarily bizarre mimicry of the flowers? The New Zealand botanists Robert Laing and Ellen Blackwell wrote:

> In tropical countries the flowers of orchids, or parts of them, show many curious resemblances to various animals. Grasshoppers, mosquitoes, dragon-flies, butterflies, swans, pelicans, the skin of the tiger and of the leopard, the eyes and teeth of the lynx, the face of the bull, the grin of the monkey, the head of the serpent, the tail of the rattlesnake, frogs, lizards, even the head of the extinct Dinotherium, are all mimicked by them.

Is it witchcraft ('eye of newt, toe of frog') that charms the enthusiast, or does the attraction signify more? John Donne could boast 'O my luve's like a red red rose', but the rose is a stolid thing when one compares it with an orchid and all the nuances of femininity that its flowers achieve.

Or is this lust for orchids based on something deeper, some secret hinted darkly in the orchid's anatomy? In the Middle Ages, European doctrine maintained that God had shown men how plants should be used medically by giving them indicative shapes. A seventeenth century *Dispensatory* translated Paracelsus: '. . . by the outward shapes and qualities of things we may know their inward Vertues, which God hath put in them for the good of man.'

The Greeks had similar notions, and this 'Doctrine of Signatures' reflected the deeply held medieval belief that the Greeks were guided by inspired medical wisdom. Thus, a heart-shaped leaf would indicate good medicine for the heart; a plant with a root shaped like a hand would be best for afflictions of the hand; one with kidney-shaped leaves effective against kidney ailments, and so on. Why else would God give them such shapes?

Many European ground orchids have testicle-shaped tubers. In curious contrast to the femininity of its flowers, the orchid's name derives from the shape of its underground parts: *orchis* is Greek for testicle. Local British names for ground orchids include 'cullions', 'ballock-grass', 'bull-bags', 'cockoo-pint', 'fool's stones', 'dog's stones' and 'fox-stones', and similar names appear in all European languages.

‡ 4 *Tragorchis minor Batauica.*
The small Goat stones of Holland.

Medieval woodcut of what is nowadays known as the lizard orchid, *Himantoglossum hircinum*. It was called the 'goats' stones', and indeed its Latin name refers to the strong perfume of billy goat given off by the flowers.

By their shape we should know their virtues. The plants were therefore (of course) used as aphrodisiacs, and medieval herbals are full of wise words on the effects of preparations made from the tubers of ground orchids on men, rams, stallions and billy goats.

The flower is the icon of woman and the tuber 'provokes lust exceedingly' in men. Pretty powerful plants. Pretty *and* powerful plants.

Collectors

The 'immortal' Joseph Banks and Daniel Solander accompanied Cook as naturalists on the first (*Endeavour*) voyage to New Zealand, and in 1769 they found eight orchids here; unfortunately Solander's manuscript descriptions were never published. The Forsters, father and son, did describe the three they found on the second (*Resolution*) voyage—*Thelymitra longifolia*, *Microtis unifolia* and *Earina autumnalis*.

Once the Church Missionary Society had set up at Kororareka, collectors began arriving in numbers: Allan Cunningham (*Pterostylis banksii*, *Earina mucronata* and *Corybas rivularis*) and his brother Richard (*Winika cunninghamii*), Joseph Dalton Hooker, Charles Darwin and John Carne Bidwill (*Earina autumnalis*), David Lyall (*Caladenia lyallii*), who was surgeon on the *Acheron*, and the French under Dumont d'Urville (*Orthoceras novae-zeelandiae*).

The period of visiting collectors ended with the publication of Hooker's *Flora Novae Zelandiae* in 1853. (The Swede Sven Berggren visited briefly and discovered *Thelymitra intermedia* in 1878, but resident collectors by now occupied the field.)

William Colenso, who had arrived at the Bay of Islands in 1834, and was to become one of the most enigmatic figures in New Zealand botany, knew orchids intimately. Colenso collected 22 of the new orchid species described by Hooker in his *Handbook of the New Zealand Flora* in 1864. He retired in 1877 at the age of 66, and from 1881 to 1898 he described 36 new orchids. His biographers, Bagnall and Peterson, wrote:

> Thus began the long series of descriptions of specimens which he alone considered to have specific validity. The specimens once described were usually sent to Kew, and there were seldom duplicates for his fellow botanists in New Zealand . . . he was as a collector the leading New Zealand figure for twenty-five years. As a taxonomist he suffered rather from lack of self-discipline than from ignorance.

> His later botanical work is marred by too wide an attention to variations in the determination of species ... Cheeseman ... rejected some 360 species of Colenso's later work.

Thomas Frederic Cheeseman would accept only two of Colenso's 36 orchids as valid species — *Bulbophyllum tuberculatum* and *Pterostylis venosa*. Since Cheeseman others have accepted *Corybas orbiculatus*, *Pterostylis patens*, *P. tristis*, *Thelymitra formosa* (*T. circumsepta*) and *T. nervosa* (*T. decora*) as true species. 'Splitting' is now a valid activity with the current refinement in taxonomic methodology, so we can expect more of Colenso's names to be resurrected.

Cheeseman arrived in Auckland in 1853, and for 50 years from 1874 was curator of the Auckland Museum. He published his *Manual of the New Zealand Flora* in 1906, with a second edition in 1925, and the massive, two-volume *Illustrations of the New Zealand Flora* in 1914. He described a number of orchid species and founded the genus *Townsonia*.

Edwin Daniel (Dan) Hatch wrote 19 papers on native orchids for the *Transactions of the Royal Society of New Zealand* between 1945 and 1963, these among a hundred of his published botanical papers. An accountant whose interest in orchids was aroused during the war when he was at Waiouru, where he discovered several new species, this 'amateur' botanist was the greatest orchidologist of his time.

The first professional woman botanist to write scientific papers about the New Zealand orchids was Ella Campbell. Her papers on the mycorrhizal fungal associations of the New Zealand saprophytic orchids are classics. She addressed the International Orchid Conference on native orchids in 1980, and became Dame Ella Campbell in 1997.

Lucy Moore was a professional botanist who collaborated with the artist Bruce Irwin to produce the orchid section of the *Flora of New Zealand* in 1970, and the *Oxford Book of New Zealand Plants* in 1978. The *Flora* is still the 'Bible' for many who await a new treatment of our orchids.

James Bruce Irwin is a man with a vast knowledge of the New Zealand orchids which he unobtrusively provides to those who are privileged to accompany him on trips into the field, and through contributions to the orchid literature. His has been a great gift.

Dorothy Cooper founded the New Zealand Native Orchid Group in 1982. She thus began a movement that has greatly increased the knowledge of native orchids among a growing number of New Zealanders. There is now a sizeable cadre of perceptive amateur and professional orchidologists who write about orchids, meet, talk, draw, photograph, contribute to the Group's *Journal*, and take part in conservation activities. They are making new discoveries every season.

Only two women have formally described New Zealand orchids: the former was Lucy Moore (*Microtis oligantha*, *Pterostylis brumalis* and *Thelymitra hatchii* and *Thelymitra* x *dentata* in 1969) and the latter was Dorothy Cooper (*Pterostylis cardiostigma* in 1983).

Brian Molloy has been the guiding professional botanist in orchid matters in the last 15 years. *Native Orchids of New Zealand*, in which John Johns' photographs were accompanied by Molloy's text, appeared in 1983, and he has described (in association with others) 10 new orchid species and two new orchid genera in New Zealand in the last few years, more than anybody since Colenso. The great taxonomic works on New Zealand orchids have been Hooker's *Flora* and his *Handbook*, Cheeseman's *Manual*, Hatch's papers in the *Transactions*, and Moore's work in the *Flora*. Work on further taxonomic refinement is currently in the hands of Brian Molloy and the Australians Mark Clements and David Jones.

Artists

When we look closely, we become aware that in the small world of botanical illustration there is a meeting of art and science, of romantic and analytical thought, of immediate appearance and underlying form.

In a review of a recent book on Albrecht Dürer, Philip Morrison wrote:

> Dürer's mastery, like Leonardo's, served natural science and art simultaneously. Thereafter the two realms drifted apart. Scientists still share the Renaissance aim of extracting meaning from its natural matrix, but the meaning they find now has lost its intimacy as science has extended its perceptual tools. Even artists today hardly cluster around direct and clear inspection, however charged their work may be with insight. All the same, one busy green enclave does remain after four centuries: flowers and birds and mammals (though not much else) are still brilliantly represented . . .

Botanical illustrations, wrote the great critic of the subject, Wilfrid Blunt, have been made by bold explorers in the cause of science and by timid spinsters to the glory of God. The American philosopher Robert Pirsig has written of romantic and analytical thought:

> What you've got here, really, are *two* realities, one of immediate artistic appearance and one of underlying scientific explanation, and they don't match and they don't fit and they don't really have much of anything to do with one another.

To the scientist, art is frivolous. To the artist, scientific analysis destroys the essence, the wholeness of the subject. Goethe lamented in 1831:

> A great flower painter is not now to be expected: we have attained too high a degree of scientific truth; and the botanist counts the stamens after the painter and has no eye for picturesque grouping and lighting.

Francis Bauer, the greatest botanical artist ever, was then nearing the end of his career. It is especially chic today to mourn the diminishing of art by science, but knowledge creates its own kind of beauty. Pirsig, in his search for quality, had more to say:

> Mark Twain's experience comes to mind, in which, after he had mastered the analytic knowledge needed to pilot the Mississippi River, he discovered the river had lost its beauty. Something is always killed. But what is less noticed in the arts, something is always created too. And instead of just dwelling on what is killed it's important also to see what's created ...

Zoologist Peter Whitehead eloquently introduced twentieth-century renaissance man:

> The artist-scientist ... is not just an illustrator. He elaborates at the interface between us and the world around us, between what we know things are and what we feel things are, and in doing so touches exactly at the point where understanding begins. We feel the truth as much as we know it.

Goethe was wrong. Keats was right: 'Beauty is truth, truth beauty'. So was William Carlos Williams: 'Are facts not flowers and flowers facts, or poems flowers, or all works of the imagination interchangeable?' The good scientist can be a good artist too; scientific illustration is the better for creativity.

Art often tells us something of the artist as well as of the subject. Compare on the one hand the clear explanatory elucidation in the illustrations of E.D. Hatch or Dorothy Cooper with, on the other, the fleshed-out pterostylis-person of Fanny Osborne, the brooding threat of Digby Graham's spider orchid, the willowy caprice of Emily Cheeseman's slender pterostylises and the dreamy whimsy of Emily Cumming Harris's flower groups.

Corybas rivularis drawn by Digby Graham, Northland, 1975. The exaggerated curves and the sinuous rounded 'tentacles' of the flower give it a threatening, reptilian appearance: is this surrealism in botanical art?

The identification of the artist and the work is so strong in our minds that we even call the work by the artist's name — we might say 'the Canterbury museum has a Margaret Stoddart of *Thelymitra pulchella*.' We would not call a scientific diagram by the name of the scientist. The scientific illustrator shows us a great deal about the subject, but little about him or herself.

Science is about reduction to a single, universally applicable, testable truth, but there is no single objective 'truth' in a work of art: there are a multitude of truths. Beauty is in the eye of the beholder as much as in that of the creator. The emotion aroused by a work of art is experienced and embellished by each observer, so the meaning may be different for each.

A few of our orchids were drawn by the great botanical masters, and many more have been subjects for New Zealand artists. Sydney Parkinson, Cook's artist on the *Endeavour* voyage, sketched eight orchids, but the plates made from his drawings were not published at the time: they appeared as *Banks's Florilegium* 200 years later.

George Forster sketched *Earina autumnalis* from Dusky Sound, and *Microtis unifolia* and *Thelymitra longifolia* from Queen Charlotte Sound when Cook's *Resolution* was there in 1773; he later prepared engravings for publication. Some dismiss him in a sentence: 'His work is far inferior to that of Parkinson,' wrote Wilfred Blunt. But others have disagreed: 'He was a natural history artist of keen and scrupulous eye,' wrote Rudiger Joppien, and the Begg brothers thought 'his botanical sketches were done with great delicacy and in the most minute detail'. William Hodges, artist on the *Resolution*, copied Forster's drawings, perhaps intending to use the plants as foreground staffage in his paintings from the voyage.

In 1826 Allan Cunningham found *Pterostylis banksii* on the bank of a stream in the Bay of Islands. He took some to Sydney, and later sent them to Kew, by which time they had died back to tubers and were presumed dead. But the next season everybody was surprised to see a perfect specimen emerge, to flower, and to be painted by Francis Bauer.

Walter Hood Fitch was artist for New Zealand's first illustrated *Flora*, the third volume of Hooker's *The Botany of Ross's Antarctic Voyage* (1844–60). Among the drawings in the *Flora Novae Zelandiae* are those of *Corybas macranthus* and *Corybas oblongus*, *Adenochilus gracilis* and a *Caladenia*. Coloured and uncoloured versions of the whole work were printed. Fitch was a superb botanical artist; his obituary said: 'Fitch had no rival for grace and fidelity to Nature. His vast experience gave him a power of perception and insight such as few, if any, artists have possessed in greater, if equal degree.'

Many women have been associated with New Zealand orchids, at first mostly as illustrators. Perhaps the earliest was a Parisienne, Eleonore Sophie Rebel. She was a burin engraver of plants, and was involved in the production of the plates of *Thelymitra longifolia* and *Orthoceras novae-zeelandiae* in the botanical atlas *Flore de la Nouvelle Zelande* of 1832, by Pierre-Adolphe Lesson and Achille Richard, who accompanied Dumont d'Urville.

John Buchanan (1818–98) was a prolific artist. Sketchbooks in Dunedin, Wellington and Auckland are full of beautiful natural history and topographical drawings. He was chief illustrator for the *Transactions of the New Zealand Institute*, and drew and engraved many of the lithographs for its first 19 volumes — 'JB del.' appears on most. His 'Milford Sound, looking North-West from Freshwater Basin' has been described as one of the masterpieces of New Zealand landscape painting. One of his sketchbooks

Francis Bauer's painting of *Pterostylis banksii* appeared in *Curtis's Botanical Magazine* in 1832.

in the Alexander Turnbull Library contains copies of the W.H. Fitch drawings of New Zealand orchids; in the *Transactions* is a curious lithograph of a plant he collected near Picton and called *Gastrodia hectori* — it was identified by Cheeseman as a *Prasophyllum*. In one of his sketchbooks in Dunedin is a watercolour of *Corybas iridescens*.

The Rev. Richard Laishley was a nonconformist minister who preached and painted in New Zealand from 1861. He was 'one of those very rare naturalists who was fully trained as an artist'. The major collection of his work remains unpublished in the British Museum (Natural History): a small notebook and two large volumes. The first, 'Gleanings of Natural History

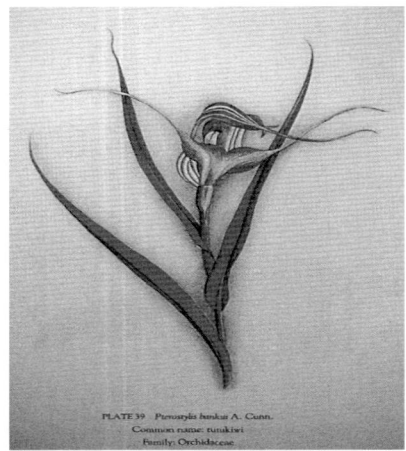 

Fanny Osborne's painting of *Pterostylis banksii* and Emily Cheeseman's *Pterostylis alobula*

in New Zealand' by R.L., several years a resident in this country (descriptions of flora and fauna), and the second, 'Notes and Drawings in New Zealand', with nearly 100 representations of birds, insects, plants, scenes and other subjects. Among the drawings are *Earina mucronata*, *Orthoceras novae-zeelandiae*, *Winika cunninghamii*, *Thelymitra longifolia*, and one showing three views of *Pterostylis banksii*, 'growing near the Hape creek, Thames'.

Sven Berggren travelled extensively in New Zealand in 1874–75. Among the plants he found was a sun orchid, *Thelymitra intermedia*, which he drew.

Emily Cheeseman drew and painted orchids, but her painting of *Pterostylis alobula* was attributed to her brother Thomas Cheeseman when it appeared as an engraving in his famous 1872 paper on the fertilisation of *Pterostylis*.

A trio of Victorian women published wonderful books of New Zealand flowers about 1890. Georgina Hetley's *The Native Flowers of New Zealand* contained illustrations of orchids, and she also sketched others (now at Kew), not developed for the book. Sarah Featon's orchid paintings were intended for a second volume of *The Art Album of New Zealand Flora*, but remain unpublished in the Museum of New Zealand. Emily Cumming Harris intended her drawings of orchids for *New Zealand Mountain Flora*, alas never published; the Turnbull Library has the originals.

Ellen Blackwell met Robert Laing on their voyage to New Zealand in 1904, and played a major, but largely unrecognised, part in the descriptive and scientific writing of Laing and Blackwell's 1906 *New Zealand Plants*. Her brother Frank was the photographer who contributed the plant photographs, and the glass plates are still held at the Auckland Museum.

The Kew artist Mathilda Smith drew the orchids for Cheeseman's *Illustrations of the New Zealand Flora* of 1914. Again, it was her engraver, John Nugent Fitch, who received the praise for the quality of the illustrations. Bruce Sampson found her original drawings in the Auckland Museum collection and acknowledged her skill as an artist for the first time in his *Early New Zealand Botanical Art*.

Many flower painters worked in the wake of the published artists: of those whose work survives in public collections are Claire Scott, and Elizabeth and Lydia Blumhardt in Whangarei and Auckland in the first decade of the twentieth century, Fanny Osborne of Great Barrier Island, Fanny Richardson (Wellington), Margaret Olrog Stoddart (Christchurch), Fanny Bertha Good (New Plymouth) and Elizabeth Hocken (Dunedin).

Then came the watercolours of Jessie Brownlee in Auckland, and those of Dunedin schoolmistress Helen Dalrymple — who published the first regional account of orchids (in Otago).

Dan Hatch's father, also E.D. Hatch, made the botanically accurate drawings of the orchids for his son's papers in the *Transactions*.

Elizabeth Johnson illustrated her sister Marguerite's books and articles. Later, Dorothy Jenkin painted and Sheila Natusch drew and wrote about Stewart Island orchids.

Hugh Wilson made stylised but accurate drawings for his *Stewart Island Plants* and Dorothy Cooper executed the drawings for her 1981 book *New Zealand Native Orchids*.

Nancy Adams worked for 40 years in Wellington as a botanical artist. Her work, published in several books and many papers, includes a number of studies of native orchids.

But it is Bruce Irwin who is our greatest orchid artist. His drawings for Lucy Moore's text in *Flora II*, papers in the *Transactions*, and in the *Oxford Book of New Zealand Plants* are accurate but lively: his plants retain the character of living things, even in the line drawings. He has published many orchid portraits since, in the papers of Brian Molloy and others, and in the Native Orchid Group's *Journal*. He is a generous contributor of a great talent.

What is special about New Zealand orchids?

New Zealand has about 120 orchid taxa, a number of which are still unnamed. Seven are epiphytes, the rest terrestrial. Several are shared with Australia, but we have four single-species endemic genera, witness to our years of isolation. Sixteen species and six unnamed taxa are listed as threatened, 10 of them regarded as endemic to New Zealand.

New Zealand's ancestral landmass, along with those of India, Australia, Africa, South America and Antarctica, had formed the great continent of Gondwana. In Jurassic times this enjoyed a temperate climate that was hospitable to the kauri, ferns, frogs, tuatara and kiwi that shared it.

At the start of the Cretaceous period the great landmass split, and early New Zealand formed a part of West Gondwana. The first angiosperms are thought to have evolved in the West Gondwana rainforests, and the sequence of division of the continent thereafter determined where ancient flowers would be established. Lilies were formed, and later, perhaps 80–100 million years ago, the first terrestrial orchids. The Tasman Sea opened up 60–80 million years ago, setting New Zealand adrift from Australia, along with its West Gondwana plants, among them some primitive orchids.

By the Eocene epoch (38–54 million years ago) flowering plants and insects were diversifying rapidly. In Australia they formed the unique plant–insect pollination partnerships seen today. In New Zealand few such partnerships developed, and most of our orchids adapted to self-pollination.

This is all guesswork of course — no orchid fossils have ever been found in any parts of old Gondwana. (Two plant fossils thought to be orchidaceous have been found in Eocene rock in Italy — *Protorchis monorchis* and *Palaeorchis rhizoma* — and orchid fruit from the Pliocene epoch 2.5–10 million years ago have been found in Germany.)

Later, dust-like orchid seed from Malaysia and Australia made effective landfall here, borne on the prevailing westerlies, sometimes accompanied by the necessary pollinating insects.

Twelve of the orchids currently regarded as threatened in New Zealand are migrants from eastern Australia, the result of seed dispersal on the prevailing west to east winds. They have remained scarce in New Zealand through their inability to reproduce here (lack of a specific pollinator) or to use successfully the range of habitats available (lack of mycorrhiza). Peter de Lange and Brian Molloy have called these orchids 'vagrants'.

What really is special about the New Zealand orchids is the ability of the majority of them to self-pollinate. In fact, in a classic paper, Brian Molloy estimated that 60 percent of our orchids are predominantly self-pollinating, a consequence, at least to some extent, of the relative scarcity of insects in New Zealand.

Another feature that at first seems unique to New Zealand orchids is their ability to adapt to new habitats under exotic forest trees. In fact, European orchids thrive under introduced pines too, as do some Australian species. What is unique to New Zealand is that in one place that 'artificial' environment is so rich in native orchid flora that a reserve has been created. In a *Pinus nigra* plantation near Taupo is the Iwitahi Native Orchid Reserve, the result of extensive negotiation and teamwork by a range of interested people led by the inspirational Trevor Nicholls. It is a living museum of central North Island orchid species.

Orchid habitats

Mr and Mrs E.H. Featon's *The Art Album of New Zealand Flora* appeared in 1889; Edward Featon wrote the text, and it was adorned with more adjectives than there were colours in his wife's paintings. Try chanting this to a descending scale:

> High in the alps of the Middle Island, amidst the clouds and snow, we find the chaste and velvetty Edelweiss, the sweet-scented Notholaspi, and the little Hectorella. Upon a lower zone the beautiful Celmisias with their well-clad shaggy foliage and conspicuous aster-like flowers, adorn the plateaux — lower still the subalpine Beeches with the luxuriant flowering Tawari, and the handsome Hoheria, break the dark lines of the primeval forest, and lower again stately trees, handsome flowering shrubs, trembling ferns, springy mosses, and hoary lichens clothe the landscape, down to the plains below, where the luxuriant tropical Nikau Palm, and the quaint Cordyline strike their roots deep into the soil.

Our orchids occupy all those habitats. I have seen *Prasophyllum colensoi* flowering well above the tree-line at 1500 m in Fiordland and *Gastrodia minor* among sedges in a brackish estuarine swamp near Invercargill.

The perching orchids can grow on rocks and fallen logs as well as on trees (on trees with smooth bark usually – flaking bark means their foothold is soon loosened). Ground orchids can be found in cups of humus in the

An alpine meadow in the Caples Valley, Otago — habitat for
Microtis oligantha. IStG

forks of trees. Our swamp orchids are *Thelymitra cyanea*, *Spiranthes sinensis*, *Prasophyllum* aff. *patens*, *Pterostylis micromega*, *P. paludosa* and *Cryptostylis subulata*. *Danhatchia australis* grows only in association with nikau and taraire. *Gastrodia cunninghamii* may grow in association with rhododendrons as well as its native partners. I have seen *Gastrodia minor* growing in association with gorse on a Queenstown track and in association with tussock in a paddock north of Dunedin.

The New Zealand orchids can be found in any conditions from dark forest to open clay banks in scorching sunlight, but these are specialised habitats, and most species prefer dappled light under scrub or at tracksides where the soil has been freshly turned. Orchids found in plenty last century (*Pterostylis nutans* and *Caleana minor*, for example) may have been here in good numbers before their habitat was disturbed, but it is just as likely they represent opportunistic colonisation when the soil of the new country was freshly turned.

Life cycle

The terrestrial orchid is a monocotyledon. From a node on its rhizome arises the flowering stem: the round tuber of *Pterostylis* is a node, and the

Aporostylis bifolia seems to inhibit the growth of *Chiloglottis cornuta* under *Pinus nigra*, Lake Mahinerangi. IStG

Earina autumnalis, Dusky Sound. IStG

root below it an internode; the oval tuber of *Thelymitra* is a node and an expanded internode; and that of *Gastrodia*, a series of nodes and internodes. The tuber is enlarged as an energy store for dormancy and regrowth.

Our epiphytes are evergreen but the terrestrials are annual plants, though *Spiranthes*, a swamp-dweller, is often perennial. *Thelymitra* leaves appear in autumn, grow rapidly in spring, and flower in spring and summer; other species emerge only weeks before flowering.

After the flowers are pollinated, the ovaries swell, and in many species the stems elongate greatly as the fruit ripens, so when dehiscence occurs and the seed is dispersed, it is released from a height (*Corybas cryptanthus* flowers beneath the leaf litter of the forest floor, and it is the elongated leafless fruiting stems protruding from the surface that betrays the presence of plants). Each fruit produces thousands of tiny seeds, each completely lacking its own nutrition: their lightness gives them the advantage of easy dispersal on the winds, but the disadvantage that they need to form an association with a fungus to provide the food for development (see page 28ff). After fungal invasion, the embryo forms what is called a protocorm, and this grows, often over several years, into the mature plant.

I know of few longitudinal studies of New Zealand orchids. Dan Hatch found that 3 mm tubers of *Pterostylis alobula*, *trullifolia* and *brumalis* formed juvenile rosettes; intermediate-sized tubers formed intermediate plants; and only when the tuber reached 7 mm diameter did an adult form emerge, to flower. The juvenile rosettes provide maximal leaf area for photosynthesis and tuber development.

In Europe, population dynamics is a complex subject. Some plants lie dormant for one or more seasons. Some emerge, but die back before the others in the colony flower, so a population count at flowering time may be inaccurate. Some flower in one season, but not in the next. In one species, the number of flowers bore a relationship to the amount of sunshine in the preceding summer. Some species appear to be long-lived, others have but brief lives.

Several Australian, South African and North American orchids require regular burns for flowering. The tubers lie dormant until stimulated by chemicals in the smoke, then the black forest comes alive with new flowers. If the burns are too infrequent, the forest litter builds up and the fires burn so fiercely the orchid tubers may be cooked. Controlled burning has been used successfully in the management of several orchid species, including New Zealand's last known population of *Corybas carsei*.

Flowers

Before discussing flowers, we should define some terms:
sepal: one part of the outer, usually greenish whorl (called the calyx) of flower parts.
petal: one part of the inner, usually showy whorl (called the corolla) of flower parts.
anther: the pollen-bearing part of the male organ which, along with the supporting stalk, forms the stamen.
stigma: the receptive part of the female organ which, along with the ovule-bearing ovary, forms the carpel (stigma and ovary connected together by a style).

Some time in the early Cretaceous period an ancestral monocotyledon developed five concentric whorls of flower parts — three sepals, outside three petals, outside three stamens, outside three carpels.

Lilies retain six stamens and three joined stigmas, but the ancestral orchid took a great evolutionary leap forward. This was the modification of most of the carpels and stamens into a single structure called the *column*. Three sepals enclose three petals, but now they twist through 180°, the lowermost petal enlarging to form the *labellum*, and the uppermost sepal forming a protective hood over the column.

The column of New Zealand orchids has a single fertile anther (unstalked stamen), and two *column-wings* formed from *staminodes* (two other barren stamens). Two of its three stigmas form a double-lobed stigma, with the third sterile and modified into a *rostellum*. The stigma is connected to a single ovary (derived from three and thus three-lobed) by the *style*. Sticky material on the rostellum forms the *viscidium* (*viscid disk*), often attached by a thin stalk, or *stipe*, to the *pollinia* (aggregated pollen).

At some stage of their evolution many of the New Zealand orchids have been insect-pollinated, and so have developed various methods of attracting insects — scent, edible *calli*, nectar or colour. Usually it is the labellum that is most modified, enlarged, colourful or lumpy, carrying nectaries or scent organs.

In *Thelymitra*, however, the labellum is little different from the other petals and sepals, and it is the tufted-column wings that attract the insects. In other genera the flower parts are modified in different ways — the labellum is rolled into a tube in *Corybas*, lies within a tube formed by the other parts in *Gastrodia*, is mobile within a tube formed by the 'zipping' together of the other flower parts in *Pterostylis*, is uppermost in the

The different shapes of the New Zealand orchids clockwise from top left: *Caladenia, Pterostylis, Gastrodia, Thelymitra.*

non-resupinate flowers (labellum uppermost) of *Prasophyllum*, *Gastrodia* and *Cryptostylis subulata*, is colourful and bedecked with calli in *Caladenia*, and colourful and hairy in *Calochilus*.

Pollination

Charles Darwin's book on orchid fertilisation first appeared in 1862, and a second edition named *The Various Contrivances by which Orchids are Fertilised by Insects* appeared in 1904. Darwin disliked the idea of self-pollination, and in the first edition of his book he wrote, 'It is hardly an exaggeration to say that Nature tells us, in the most emphatic manner, that she abhors perpetual self-fertilisation.'

One can trace a gradual softening of Darwin's stance on the subject: from evident incredulity bordering on disgust that self-pollination was even possible in the early 1860s, through to acceptance 15 years later that it happened, though obviously only when normal, healthy cross-pollination by insects had somehow failed, and then only temporarily. In the early seventies he would list the orchid species in which 'self-fertilisation habitually occurs', but would add:

> I believe that the few orchids which do not now intercross, either did formerly intercross, or that they will do so at some future period under different conditions, unless, indeed, they become extinct from the evil effects of long-continued close interbreeding.

The great Australian orchidologist Robert Desmond FitzGerald wrote, in a famous preface in 1876:

> Mr. Darwin's proposition regarding 'the contrivances by which Orchids are fertilized' is, that they 'have for their main objects the fertilization of each flower by the pollen of another flower.' As far as I could investigate the subject in Australia, I have not been able altogether to verify this proposition; for though the great majority appear to be frequently impregnated by pollen brought from other flowers, I believe they are also frequently fertilized by their own . . .

Darwin doubted the accuracy of FitzGerald's observations on the self-pollination of *Spiranthes*, suggesting that it should be ascertained whether insects *ever* visit the flowers.

With few exceptions, if pollination is to take place the pollen from the male anther must come into contact with the female stigma. As with other flowers, insects may help in this. Perhaps 97 percent of the world's orchids are indeed insect-pollinated. But in New Zealand the position appears to be quite different. Perhaps 60 percent of New Zealand orchids show autogamy, or self-pollination.

Captain James Cook wrote in 1776, after his third visit to New Zealand:

> Insects are very rare. Of these, we only saw two sorts of dragon-flies, some butterflies, small grass-hoppers, several sorts of spiders, some small black ants, and vast numbers of scorpion-flies, with whose chirping the woods resound.

Brian Molloy compared the reported insect faunas of Australia and New Zealand and reached the same conclusion: paucity of insects is, at least to some extent, associated with self-pollination.

Many self-pollinating species have been derived from insect-pollinated ancestors, and still show some of the anatomical structures that suggest insect pollination. These characteristics that suggest insect pollination include many that Darwin observed (see table). Such characteristics do not necessarily prove insect-pollination.

Apart from the field commentaries of G.M. Thomson and T.F. Cheeseman at around the turn of the century, few observations on the pollination of New Zealand orchids have been carried out, but characteristics that suggest predominant self-pollination are shown in the table.

We have often, in New Zealand, rather coyly talked of the pale and 'delicate' beauty of our flowers, which others have been cruel enough to call 'inconspicuous'; we don't have the masses of colour of a Swiss alpine meadow — but then neither do we have to wear leather pants to keep the stinging insects at bay.

Thelymitra longifolia buds often remain steadfastly closed, and after a while one becomes aware that the ovary is swelling, and the flower will never open. Cheeseman wrote of *T. longifolia* that the two anther cells split to expose the pollinia when the bud is still closed, and that these pollinia adhere to the sticky upper surface of the rostellum. The column then lengthens so the anther-case leaves the pollinia hanging there in the narrow space between stigma and column.

> The upper part of the stigma is thin and membranous, and has its margin slightly revolute, even when in bud. After expansion (of the flower) this rolling back is carried to a greater extent, so that the edge of the stigma, and even a small portion of its anterior surface, comes into contact with the pollen masses hanging directly behind it.

Signs suggesting insect-pollination	**Signs suggesting self-pollination**
Many large colourful flowers open wide and long (*Winika cunninghamii*);	Small, few flowers (*Gastrodia minor*, *Microtis oligantha*) never, barely or only briefly open (*Bulbophyllum pygmaeum*);
Flowers produce nectar or scent (*Earina autumnalis*);	Flowers do not produce nectar or scent;
A large, colourful (*Aporostylis bifolia*) or irritable labellum (*Pterostylis banksii*) acts as a landing platform;	Flowers may be non-resupinate (labellum uppermost) (*Prasophyllum colensoi*, *Genoplesium nudum*) or lack a conspicuous labellum (*Waireia stenopetala*);
Pollen forms adherent masses called pollinia (*Thelymitra* aff. *longifolia*);	Pollen is noncoherent or mealy and falls easily onto the stigma (*Thelymitra pulchella*);
Anther and stigma are widely separated (*Gastsrodia* aff. *sesamoides*);	Pollen-bearing anther is close to stigma (*Gastrodia cunninghamii*);
A prominent rostellum forms a barrier between anther and stigma (*Acianthus sinclairii*);	Flowers lack a prominent rostellum (*Waireia stsenopetala*);
A floral stance, often leaning forward, would cause falling pollen to miss a stigma that is flat and narrow (*Pterostylis nutans*);	A floral stance, often with a vertical column, would allow pollen to fall easily onto the stigma, which may be prominent (*Pterostylis cardiostigma*);
May produce scant seed;	Produce plentiful seed;
Because of cross-pollination individuals within a species may show local variation to the extent they may be mistaken for different species.	Because of the inbreeding that self-pollination implies, individuals in a geographical region tend to show little intra-specific variation.

> Pollen-tubes are at once emitted into the substance of the stigma, usually so rapidly that before a flower has been expanded more than a single day the pollinia are glued so firmly to the margin of the stigma that they could not be removed by insects, even if they visited the flowers.

There is also another mechanism for self-pollination — penetration of the stigma from behind. Bruce Irwin observed this and wrote:

> The pollinia of *Orthoceras novae-zeelandiae* were said to be 'ill-defined', so I made careful drawings of them. When I tipped the anther back, the pollinia were withdrawn because they were cemented to the back of the stigma, presumably by germinating pollen tubes. This suggested that pollen tubes penetrate through the *back* of the stigma.

Charles Darwin did suggest that self-pollination may be a fall-back position adopted by species that are normally insect-pollinated, and he even admitted that self-pollination was better than extinction.

The advantages of cross-pollination over self-pollination may have been exaggerated. There may be other methods of achieving variety in the gene pool.

'Lower' organisms that reproduce asexually have built-in safeguards to achieve it. The influenza virus keeps ahead of our human immune systems by mutating every few years; the yeast *Candida albicans*, which causes thrush, also mutates easily, with the transfer of genetic material during mitosis. We don't know about higher plants, and indeed the uniformity of structure in self-pollinating orchids in contemporaneous populations (along with the fact that they still retain now useless insect attractants) might suggest that such genetic change is uncommon.

But clearly there has been modification in some of our orchids since their ancestors left Australia, and that change has even occurred in species that were self-pollinating in that country — the New Zealand *Corybas cheesemanii* has evolved from its cousin the Australian *C. aconitiflorus*, for example.

Fungi

If you read about orchids you can't escape phrases like 'fungal associations', and 'leaf litter rich in fungal hyphae'. In fact, the roots of most vascular plants have evolved in association with soil fungi. The resulting combined structures are called mycorrhizas (literally 'fungus-roots'). Fungal invasion of animals and plants is detected by the appearance of threadlike structures called hyphae in the tissues.

Whereas medical mycologists identify pathogenic fungi by their asexual spores, plant mycologists may deal with fungi that develop perfect states — the fruit that contain sexual spores — and use these for identification. Where perfect states cannot be achieved in cultivation, the structure of the hyphae, the pattern of branching and rejoining of hyphae (anastomosis), or the number of nuclei in cells may give a clue as to identity.

The habitat of the fungus may determine the habitat of the orchid — thus the fungus *Rhizoctonia borealis* requires acid soils under conifers, so that is where its associated European orchids *Spiranthes gracilis* and *Goodyera repens* are found.

Strictly, the term mycorrhiza should apply only to the fungus/root association, but it is loosely applied also to the association between the fungus and the developing orchid protocorm (the stage between seed and embryo).

Orchids require the relationship with a fungus for their existence. The importance differs among species, the 'infection' by the fungus being heaviest in temperate terrestrials but light in tropical epiphytes. The relationship is essential for the germination of the seed of all orchids in the wild, and remains essential for a few species throughout life.

Orchid seeds are tiny and lack the built-in nutrition of bigger seeds; orchids then pass through a non-green ('achlorophyllous') developmental stage when they cannot use fats, break down starch, obtain phosphates or photosynthesise, and therefore rely on an external source. This is provided either by man in the form of simple carbon-containing foods in sterile seed germination on special culture media, or by a fungus which breaks down complex compounds into simpler ones in symbiotic germination. The fungal hyphae penetrate via the base end of the seed. The hyphae enter the cells and coil into structures called pelotons. Germination of the seed into a protocorm follows. The cells eventually digest the pelotons, but occasionally the fungi become parasitic and destroy the protocorm.

In some plants (*Gastrodia*, *Danhatchia* and *Corybas cryptanthus* in New Zealand) chlorophyll never does develop, so the orchids rely for all their lives on associations with fungi. In others, the leaf-size is too small to support the rest of the orchid, and the orchid continues to rely partly on the fungus for its nutrition (*Corybas cheesemanii*, for instance); such plants have been called saprophytic, but that is an incorrect application of the term. Some plants of the European *Spiranthes spiralis* pass alternate seasons underground, apparently fully nourished by their fungus during that time.

The partnership between orchid and fungus has been called symbiosis (a 'win-win situation'), or a 'delicately balanced mutual antagonism' as Joseph Arditti called it, or plain parasitism (of the orchid on the fungus, that is). 'Symbiosis' suggests mutual benefit, and indeed *Cymbidium* and its fungus each require the vitamin thiamine, made up of thiazole and pyridine; the fungus supplies the thiazole and the orchid supplies the pyridine. Most orchid-associated fungi can, however, live without the orchid, and it seems that whereas the fungus supplies the orchid with a range of nutrients and stimuli, the orchid usually provides little in return.

Fungi that are apparently symbiotic can turn nasty and attack the orchid; furthermore, the fungi of epiphytes may invade the orchid's host tree, to the tree's (and ultimately the orchid's) detriment.

Some laboratory studies suggest that specific orchids require specific fungi, but few associations have been studied in the wild, fungi are difficult to isolate and difficult to grow (especially to the usually identifiable perfect state), and even in one orchid, the fungus required by the protocorm may be different from that required by the adult. Certainly some orchids can establish successful relations with several different fungi.

Perkins has looked at the Australian orchids *Pterostylis acuminata* and *Microtis parviflora* in the wild and in the laboratory. Whereas only a few species of fungi were associated in the wild, several more would form associations in the laboratory — thus 'ecological specificity' (what happens in the wild) is different from 'potential specificity' (what *could* happen if laboratory experiments were to reflect the wild state).

In New Zealand, in 1911, Lancaster showed that fungal hyphae do penetrate the root hairs of New Zealand epiphytes and form pelotons which are digested by the orchid cells. Ella Campbell began a series of papers on the fungal associations of New Zealand's non-green orchids in 1962; she showed:

- *Gastrodia cunninghamii* is associated with the fungus *Armillaria mellea*, which is itself a parasite on the roots of forest trees;
- *G. minor* is associated with and derives nutrients from an unidentified fungus which also penetrates the roots of adjacent manuka;
- What is probably the bracket fungus *Fomes mastoporus* inhabits the roots of *Acacia melanoxylon* and is an endophyte of *Gastrodia* aff. *sesamoides*, which digests it;

- All around the roots of taraire trees grow the hyphae of the puffball fungus *Lycoperdon perelatum*, and these hyphae form a network around and attach to the rhizomes of *Danhatchia australis*, invade the tips of root hairs, and are digested by the cells of the orchid.
- *Corybas cryptanthus* has an associated unidentified fungus that invades the roots through root hairs attached at tiny conical projections; the fungus spreads among the beech-leaf litter, and is a weak parasite on the *Nothofagus*.

Jack Warcup, Mark Clements, Kingsley Dixon, A. Perkins and their co-workers have been the major contributors in Australia to the study of orchid/fungus relationships. Here are a few snippets.

- Warcup and Talbot grew fungi from pelotons teased from the cells of Australian native orchids — of 102 isolates from 25 orchid species, 66 fungi were induced to fruit. Fungal species of the following genera formed mycorrhizal associations with orchids (of the genera in brackets): *Thanatophorous (Acianthus, Thelymitra), Ceratobasidium (Pterostylis, Prasophyllum, Acianthus), Tulasnella (Diuris, Acianthus, Thelymitra, Caladenia, Cymbidium, Dendrobium)* and *Sebacina (Acianthus, Caladenia, Glossodia, Microtis)*; the same fungal species often formed mycorrhizal associations with individual European orchids. These truly intracellular fungi were often different from those found on the surface of orchid roots.
- Fire affected the abundance, behaviour and composition of fungus infecting West Australian orchids.
- Initial contact between fungus and seed is haphazard — there is no evidence that an attractant is used by the orchid seed. Seeds appeared to resist entry by incompatible fungi, while allowing the entry of compatible fungi.
- In *Pterostylis* where fungi are found is determined by the environment. One fungus was found only under *Pinus radiata*. Geographic distribution of orchid species may thus be determined by fungal ecology.
- Perkins and co-workers found only two fungi associated with *Microtis parviflora* in the wild. On the other hand, many fungi were able to form associations with *M. parviflora* in the laboratory, indicating a broad potential specificity.
- The germination of orchid seed in the wild should depend on the amount of fungus in the soil, but this may not be so. Perkins and co-workers studied *Pterostylis acuminata* and its fungal associations: this orchid appears

to associate with only one specific fungus, a subspecies of *Rhizoctonia solani*. Furthermore this orchid reproduces asexually (i.e. essentially by cloning). The orchid and the fungus may therefore be co-distributed, and if an orchid is able to establish at a new site, the resultant increase in the associated fungus may favour further spread of the orchid. There are implications here for the resiting of rare orchids — if there is a single fungus associated with the orchid, a new site will need to be apt for the fungus as well as for the orchid: if the fungus does not survive, neither will the orchid.

Orchids that form ecologically specific relationships with single pollinating insects can only survive in the presence of that specific insect. We now see that there are orchids which form ecologically specific relationships with single mycorrhizal fungi: they can only survive in the presence of that specific fungus.

Whether these observations apply to the New Zealand orchids is of course open to speculation.

Names

Common names are, by definition, names people use commonly. For the most part it is common things that people name — they only name rare things when they are dangerous, delicious or otherwise perceived as important.

None of our orchids are savage or (at least since European settlement) regarded as especially tasty. Few individual species are common enough to have earned common names (the lady's slipper, *Winika cunninghamii*, is one, although it should be noted that in Europe the lady's slipper is a *Cypripedium*), although some genera certainly are: the greenhoods, *Pterostylis*; the sun orchids, *Thelymitra*; the spider orchids, *Corybas* (although again, in Australia spider orchids are *Caladenia*).

Over the years writers have applied common words to many orchids. Their intention is noble but misplaced: the invention of artificial 'common' names increases neither familiarity with, nor love of, orchids. Those things take time. I have never heard *Pterostylis oliveri* called 'Oliver's greenhood', *Drymoanthus adversus* 'the little green forest orchid', or *Caladenia* aff. *carnea* 'pink fingers'; these are the silly inventions of underemployed minds. The scientific names may at first stall those unfamiliar with them, but in the end everybody who wants to communicate about orchids learns them and uses them in common speech. In this book I have mentioned common names only where they are justified by common use. Maori names are given below.

Botanical names have two parts — the first is the name of the genus (generic), the second that of the species (specific). Some of the generic and specific names of our orchids honour great men, others draw attention to special characteristics of the genus or species. The derivations of the generic and specific names are given on page 167.

The French call plants that have yet to be formally named *les belles inconnues*. It's a phrase that hints elegantly at beauty and mystery. Here unnamed taxa may be referred to by their resemblance to a named species (e.g. *Pterostylis* aff. *montana* — a *Pterostylis* with affinities to *P. montana*). They may also be tag-named for easy reference — for their location (*Thelymitra* 'Whakapapa', *Pterostylis* 'Catlins'), or by an anatomical feature (*Corybas* 'roundleaf', *C.* 'whiskers'). A tag-name hypothesises a distinct taxon; the use of tag-names may be deprecated by professional botanists, and it should be stated here that not all the tag-names used in this book represent plants that have been accepted by those involved in the systematic study of the New Zealand orchids. Nonetheless, while I acknowledge the arguments for caution, I believe there is more to be gained than lost by identifying plants that appear to be distinct as early as possible in the long process of scientific scrutiny. Such identification draws attention to the hypothesis and assists the process of classification by the consequent speedier acquisition of new data.

New Zealand orchids are in the process of intense scientific scrutiny, and several of the taxa named here are likely to be renamed in the near future.

Maori and orchids

J.D. Hooker listed 'native and vernacular names' for the New Zealand plants, and in 1880, William Colenso wrote of the vegetable foods of the Maori:

> Another fleshy root, and that a tolerably large one, of the Orchis family, often the size of a middling-sized kumara, or of a stout, long-red radish root — the perei (*Gastrodia cunninghamii*) — was also eaten; but it was rather scarce, and only found in dense forests.

Elsdon Best would expand on Colenso's observations in 1898:

> ... when digging for the *perei*, an edible root (*Orthoceras solandri*) the diggers must not mention the name *perei*, or the root will never be found. At such a time it is termed *maikaika*.

This was one of a number of ways in which food-gathering might fail, called generally puhore. Thus, 'when going a-hunting, should you speak of the game as already caught . . . nothing will be taken during your hunt'. Perei meant the orchid tuber as one ate it — cleaned, dried, roasted, or whatever — while maikaika referred to the plant itself.

Best would write later that the perei was *Gastrodia cunninghamii* and:

> Some singular notions prevail among the natives in regard to the *perei*. It did not, according to the Maori, originate in or from the earth, but was formed by the gods . . . The *perei* was dug in the winter season, and dried by exposure, as fern-root is. It was either roasted at a fire, or cooked in a steam-oven. It was not found in any quantity, but would be dug up when seen.

Thomas Cheeseman added to Hooker's list, and Lucy Moore noted other Maori names.

For the most part the orchids were named for their food value, although the epiphytes and *P. banksii* were named for their appearance:

Epiphytes, hiri turiti: hiri = rely, lean; turi = water.

B. pygmaeum, piripiri: piri = stick, adhere, cling; be attached to; a closely woven mat.

E. autumnalis, raupeka: rau = leaf; peka = branch (raupeka as a verb means to droop).

E. mucronata, peka-a-waka: peka = branch; a = of; waka = bird (but also canoe, etc.).

G. cunninghamii, maukuuku: ma = white; uku = fish (but see below under *O. novae-zeelandiae*); para, perei uhiperei, huperei when prepared for food (uhi, uwhi = yam).

M. unifolia, maikaika; *O. novae-zeelandiae*, ikaika, mamaika, maikaika, makaika: ma = white; ika = fish. It is difficult to know which of the several uses of ma and ika are meant here. The partial or complete duplication of a word, in this case ika, generally diminishes the intensity of the meaning; thus wera = hot, werawera = rather hot. Does ikaika mean '[tastes] rather fishy'? Para, perei when prepared for food; parareka (which also means potato), reka = palatable; paratarere = with a mottled skin; para kehe = large; para ponaho = small; paratawhiti = the para of Tahiti?

P. banksii, tutukiwi: tutu = stand erect (thus tutukiwi = standing kiwi).

T. longifolia, maikuku.

T. pulchella, maikaika.

W. cunninghamii, winika.

The maps

The distribution maps result from the New Zealand Native Orchid Group's Mapping Scheme, which includes observations since 1972. Reports of orchid finds were applied to the map of New Zealand ecological regions. While the smaller ecological districts would more accurately reflect habitat, the sheer number of districts was so much greater than the number of people reporting, that we decided to use the larger regions. Report forms were collated and the data transferred to computer-generated maps. There are inevitably distortions, omissions and inaccuracies in such a scheme. For instance where an orchid was reported from a region, the whole region is shaded (e.g. *Caleana minor* was reported from only one spot in Rotorua, but the whole region is shaded). Some species have been 'split' since the scheme began — for instance *Caladenia carnea*, as reported by Lucy Moore in 1970, contained what we now recognise as perhaps six different taxa. These changes came too late to be included in the Mapping Scheme, so maps are incomplete for such taxa. Others, such as *Corybas trilobus*, contain several other taxa, as yet unsplit, so the maps show the total distribution. Some ecological regions are remote; others were simply not reported. Most inaccuracies are likely to be omissions — under-reporting rather than misidentification. The maps should be interpreted as saying no more than: 'This taxon has been reported since 1972 from this ecological region.' For some uncommon orchids I have simply described the distribution rather than including maps for all taxa.

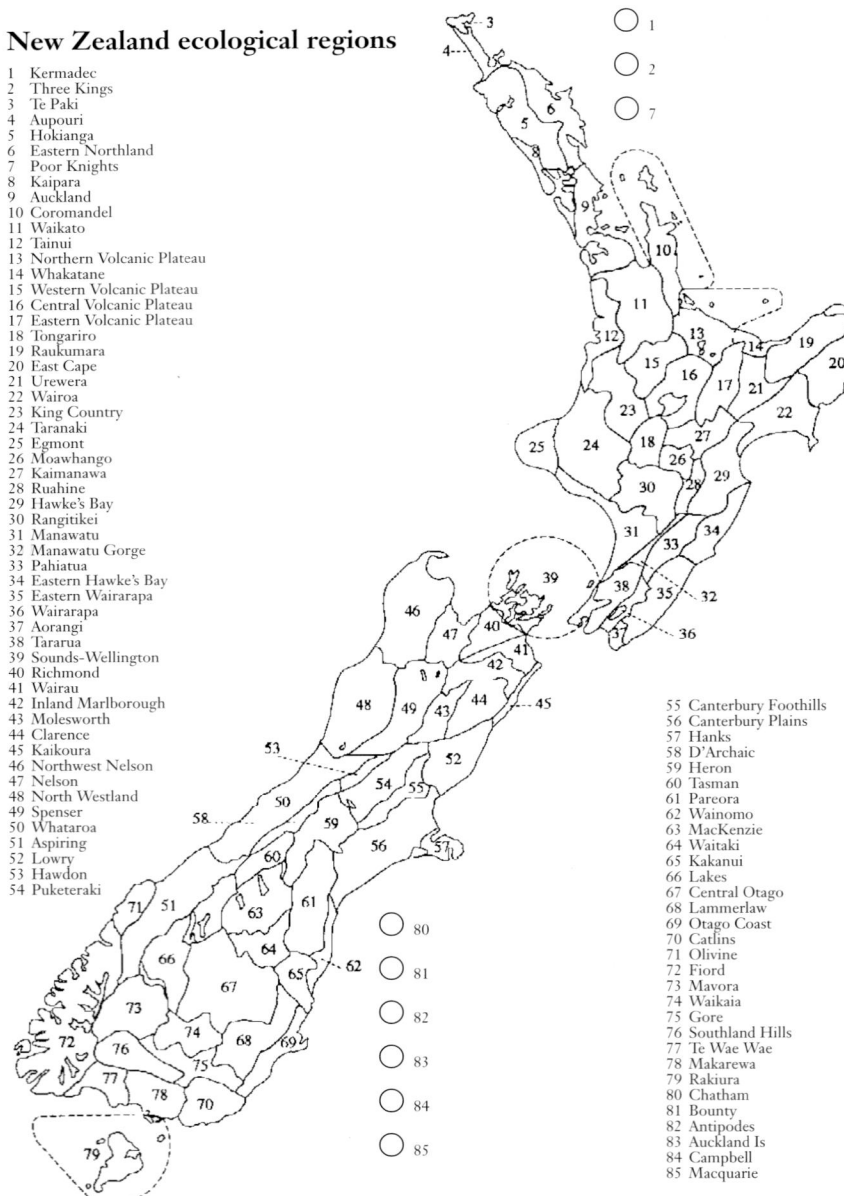

New Zealand ecological regions

1 Kermadec
2 Three Kings
3 Te Paki
4 Aupouri
5 Hokianga
6 Eastern Northland
7 Poor Knights
8 Kaipara
9 Auckland
10 Coromandel
11 Waikato
12 Tainui
13 Northern Volcanic Plateau
14 Whakatane
15 Western Volcanic Plateau
16 Central Volcanic Plateau
17 Eastern Volcanic Plateau
18 Tongariro
19 Raukumara
20 East Cape
21 Urewera
22 Wairoa
23 King Country
24 Taranaki
25 Egmont
26 Moawhango
27 Kaimanawa
28 Ruahine
29 Hawke's Bay
30 Rangitikei
31 Manawatu
32 Manawatu Gorge
33 Pahiatua
34 Eastern Hawke's Bay
35 Eastern Wairarapa
36 Wairarapa
37 Aorangi
38 Tararua
39 Sounds-Wellington
40 Richmond
41 Wairau
42 Inland Marlborough
43 Molesworth
44 Clarence
45 Kaikoura
46 Northwest Nelson
47 Nelson
48 North Westland
49 Spenser
50 Whataroa
51 Aspiring
52 Lowry
53 Hawdon
54 Puketeraki
55 Canterbury Foothills
56 Canterbury Plains
57 Hanks
58 D'Archaic
59 Heron
60 Tasman
61 Pareora
62 Wainomo
63 MacKenzie
64 Waitaki
65 Kakanui
66 Lakes
67 Central Otago
68 Lammerlaw
69 Otago Coast
70 Catlins
71 Olivine
72 Fiord
73 Mavora
74 Waikaia
75 Gore
76 Southland Hills
77 Te Wae Wae
78 Makarewa
79 Rakiura
80 Chatham
81 Bounty
82 Antipodes
83 Auckland Is
84 Campbell
85 Macquarie

NEW ZEALAND NATIVE ORCHIDS A–Z

ACIANTHUS

There are about 30 species of *Acianthus* worldwide, from New Guinea, Solomon Islands, New Caledonia and Australia. New Zealand has one, though some taxonomists include *Cyrtostylis* in *Acianthus*.

Acianthus sinclairii

This is a tiny 2–10 cm ground orchid, with a slender, square stem bearing a heart-shaped leaf. It has 1–10 green and red flowers that are less than a centimetre long. The leaves range from pale green to purple and the flowers to deep maroon. The dorsal sepal is cupped over the column; the sepals are

Acianthus sinclairii. IStG

Acianthus sinclairii. IStG

pointed; the petals are shorter, the labellum broad, cupped and pointed.

For many years thought to be a variety of the Australian *A. fornicatus*, *A. sinclairii* is now recognised as a New Zealand endemic. It is common everywhere in New Zealand except in Southland and Otago, though it has long been known from Stewart Island. Local populations are common elsewhere in New Zealand, with colonies of many plants in lowland forest and track-sides, flowering from May to October.

A. sinclairii is predominantly insect-pollinated: the prominent bilobed rostellum separates the pollinia from the stigma and prevents self-pollination.

J.D. Hooker noted in 1853 in his *Flora Novae Zelandiae*:

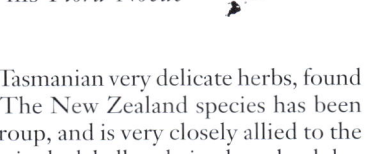

> A small genus of Australian and Tasmanian very delicate herbs, found in many places in deep woods. The New Zealand species has been found also in Lord Auckland's group, and is very closely allied to the Australian *A. fornicatus*, but differs in the labellum being less glandular.

ADENOCHILUS

Two species are recognised, one in New Zealand, the other in Australia. They are terrestrial orchids which usually have a single flower. The dorsal sepal is above, arched over the column; the lateral sepals and petals are long and thin; the labellum is semi-erect, bearing rows of calli; the column is long and curved, with wings extending above the anther; the pollinia are mealy; the stigma prominent. The leaf is single, on the flowering stem and arising at a distance from the rhizome, which is branched and fleshy.

Adenochilus gracilis. ES

Adenochilus gracilis

• Chatham

Most New Zealand ground orchids have tubers that store energy in the form of starch; *Adenochilus* is unusual in having no such tuber.

The flower is graceful, with long, pointed petals and sepals (the petals in some plants curling behind the flower almost to form a circle), the dorsal sepal arched over and nearly hiding the column and labellum. It is white or greenish, the labellum often bearing red blotches or bars, the petals sometimes similarly sparsely red-spotted. Yellow calli lie along the pointed midlobe of the labellum, which curves down and back.

The flower is 1–2 cm in diameter, single, on a long thin stem with one rather broad, pointed, triangular leaf about halfway up the stem (other leaves may be found at some distance from the plant, connected by the horizontal rhizome).

An orchid of the beech forests, found beside many bush tracks, it is also established and enjoying the rich needle humus beneath old *Pinus nigra* plantations. Common south of Taupo, it flowers December to January and is predominantly self-pollinating.

The Dunedin teacher G.M. Thomson wrote in the *Journal of Science* in 1882:

> I found the plant this last January, when botanising in the neighbourhood of Lake Hauroto (Howloko), in the south-eastern corner of the South Island . . . Mr. Petrie informs me that he believes it occurs in the forest at the head of Lake Wakatipu, but he has only seen the leaf.

APOROSTYLIS

This is an endemic New Zealand genus of one (perhaps 2) taxa.

Aporostylis bifolia

The 'odd-leaved orchid' owes its common name to the difference in size of its 2 leaves. It is a ground orchid, often preferring damp sites, about 15 cm tall, hairy-stemmed, with its 2 hairy basal leaves horizontal and unequal. In dark beech forest they may be entirely green, up to 25 cm long; in the open sun they are shorter and broader, blotched with brown. The flower is a couple of centimetres across, white, the dorsal sepal broad and somewhat arched over the green-speckled column, the other sepals and petals narrower. The labellum has yellow/brown markings, and broadens from a narrow base. As with many orchids, an occasional colony has plants with petiolate labella — an isolated colony with a narrow labellum grows at one site in the Catlins.

I have seen *A. bifolia* 3 m up the mossy trunks of trees in high rainfall forests. Its habitat ranges from upland sphagnum bogs to damp, shady, mossy forest floors to dry scrub or tussock grassland. It is locally common, flowers in January, and is predominantly insect-pollinated.

William Colenso found it in the Ruahines, and called it *Caladenia macrophylla* in 1895, writing: 'A plant that has caused me much trouble as to fixing its proper genus.' Indeed, it has been included in *Caladenia* and in *Chiloglottis*, but was finally named *Aporostylis* by Rupp and Dan Hatch in 1946.

• Chatham
• Auckland Is.
• Campbell

Opposite: *Aporostylis bifolia*. YC, IStG

BULBOPHYLLUM

There are over one thousand bulbophyllums, all perching orchids, in America, Africa and Asia. New Zealand has 2 species. This is the only New Zealand genus with a pseudobulb, the swollen leaf-base characteristic of many overseas and cultivated orchids.

Bulbophyllum pygmaeum

This 'bulb-leaf orchid' is tiny, a series of match-head sized green pseudobulbs each topped by a single, 1 cm, oval leaf, the whole plant forming a mat on branches and boles of trees (usually found when rimu or other podocarps

Bulbophyllum pygmaeum. IStG

Bulbophyllum pygmaeum. ES

fall), and on rocks. The flower is green, and 3 mm across. It opens only briefly, if at all (some buds appear to develop fruit without ever opening). It is self-pollinating, and flowers in the summer.

B. pygmaeum is rare in the south, more common in the north. It is found on treetops in Canterbury, but lower down in the north, and in the lower South Island there are records only from south Westland; it has been found occasionally on Stewart Island.

This was one of the 7 orchids found by Banks and Solander on Cook's first voyage, and illustrated by Sydney Parkinson. Solander called it 'Epidendrum pygmaeum'. Sheila Natusch made the first discovery of the species on Stewart Island, reporting in 1968:

> When I tramped across the Island to the rugged headlands in the north-west, I found, matted on a huge boulder, a creeping plant whose tiny green leaves sat on globular storage-tanks (pseudobulbs) the size of mikimik' berries, only green. This was a species of the orchid *Bulbophyllum.*

Bulbophyllum tuberculatum

This is rather larger than *B. pygmaeum*, its pear-shaped pseudobulbs smooth in youth, wrinkling with age, 1 cm x 3 mm, often more or less covered with white, waxy flakes. It favours New Zealand conifers and grows in association with lichen, forming colonies of tight clumps. The leaf is rather erect and up to 4 cm long. It bears a raceme of 2–4 whitish or cream flowers, 4 mm across, with an orange labellum. The ovary carries rows of tubercles, and the flower parts are similarly warty, hence the specific name. Flowering is in the autumn, April to May.

William Colenso first described this orchid from a flowerless specimen near Petane, Hawke's Bay, in 1884. He had to wait another 6 years to see the flower, a specimen sent to him by Augustus Hamilton from 'woods near Palmerston, County of Manawatu, April 1889'.

Bulbophyllum tuberculatum. ES

CALADENIA

Taxonomists are reclassifying the hundred or so caladenias, most of which are Australian. Only 7 of at least 10 New Zealand taxa have been described. They are hairy terrestrial orchids, with one or few flowers, the dorsal sepal standing erect or forming a hood above and the petals and lateral sepals similar to each other; the labellum is semi-erect, sometimes 3-lobed, its midlobe margins often toothed, bearing calli in longitudinal rows; the column is long and winged with a terminal anther, the 4 pollinia contain granular pollen; the tubers are globular; the single leaf is hairy, long and thin.

Caladenia alata

This is a hairy plant, up to 12 cm tall, but tending to be more robust in damp places. The flower is usually single and may be white to pink, mauve or red. The midlobe of the labellum has a single large orange callus on either side at the base and an orange patch at the tip, which is often recurved, so hiding the patch. The labellum disc is often red-barred and has 2 rows of yellow-topped calli. The leaf is long and thin. It is a plant of the Northland gumscrub, and flowers August to September. Robert Brown described this species in 1810, noting 'labellar glands in two rows, the base of the midlobe with a single tooth on either side, disc without glands'.

Caladenia alata. ES

NEW ZEALAND NATIVE ORCHIDS 47

Caladenia atradenia

This species has been called *C. carnea* var. *minor* forma *calliniger*, and has been confused with the Australian *C. iridescens*. These are tall hairy plants, dark red/green overall, with similarly coloured hairy backs to the flower parts. The dorsal sepal is sharply bent forward over the column, the labellum disc and calli are all a dark red/brown. There are 2 rows of calli (in contrast to *C. iridescens*, which has 4). The habitat is in poor soils often with moss and rushes in scrub and well-lit forest floor, Nelson to Northland; it flowers September to December.

Henry Blencoe Matthews collected this plant in the early 1900s, and described it in an unpublished manuscript as 'Caladenia calliniger'. He wrote of the labellum:

> Lamina with 2 rows of stalked club-headed calli between the lateral lobes, then more or less crowded with fig-shaped calli to near the point. The anterior lobe and all the calli, dark maroon or nearly black, the posterior portion and column blocked with magenta markings.

Caladenia atradenia. ES

48 NEW ZEALAND NATIVE ORCHIDS

Caladenia bartlettii

The flower is usually solitary, its petals and sepals crimson, pink or magenta, fading to white near the centre. The labellum has very deep lateral lobes, its tip and the tops of the calli bright yellow. The column-wings are wide. The midlobe is trough-shaped with wavy margins. It flowers September to November, and has so far been found in New Zealand only in the vicinity of the kauri. Frank Bartlett sent Dan Hatch specimens in 1947, and the latter acknowledged this in naming the plant *Caladenia carnea* var. *bartlettii*, noting: 'The writer is glad to be able to acknowledge Mr. Frank W. Bartlett, of Silverdale, whose knowledge of the gumlands flora has made his home the mecca of Auckland enthusiasts for many years.'

Caladenia bartlettii. ES

Caladenia aff. *carnea*

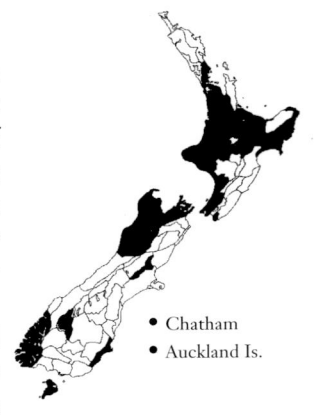
• Chatham
• Auckland Is.

The usually lone flower is a centimetre in diameter on a slender, somewhat hairy, upright stem of perhaps 15 cm. The single narrow leaf is about the same length but usually lies along the ground. The flower is most often a rich pink, a bright gem against the drab leaf litter under scrub, although it may be white or greenish.

The labellum is barred red and white, and the yellow calli in 2 more or less even rows do not extend onto the triangular midlobe; the midlobe has serrated edges and its tip is pale. The 3 sepals and the other 2 petals are long, narrow and more or less pointed, the dorsal sepal more or less upright.

C. aff. *carnea* is found here and there throughout the country (there may be more than one similar taxon, including one tagged 'big pink' under exotic pines at Iwitahi), but is nowhere common. It flowers in November and is predominantly self-pollinating. (It was once confused with *C. catenata*, but this species is now regarded as R. Brown's *C. alba* and is said to be absent from New Zealand.)

Helen Dalrymple rallied her schoolgirls on an outing in Dunedin in 1937:

> But the rarest little orchid on Stony Hill has so far evaded us. It is a very slender pink-flowered plant called *Caladenia minor*, and the girl who first finds it is to have threepence as a reward!

She was referring to *C.* aff. *carnea*, still to be found at the same site on Signal Hill today.

• Three Kings

Caladenia chlorostyla

A small terrestrial plant of the beech forests and scrub, 15–20 cm tall, the hairy red or green stem usually bearing one, though often 2 or more white to pale green flowers, the dorsal sepal forming a hood close to the labellum. The anther cap is apple-green. The labellum has a much

Caladenia aff. *carnea* ('big pink', Iwitahi). ES

Caladenia chlorostyla. IStG

longer midlobe than that of *C.* aff. *carnea* and bears prominent marginal calli; the labellum and column are red-barred. The petals and lateral sepals point more or less downwards. It flowers September to December, and is predominantly self-pollinating. A form with 2–5 flowers with dark maroon columns grows in the Rimutakas.

H.B. Matthews wrote an unpublished manuscript describing what he first called 'Caladenia viridis' and later called 'C. chloroleuca': 'A handsome little species plentiful in places north of Auckland in forest or old *Leptospermum* scrub.' The description fits this species, which was known informally as *Caladenia* 'green column' for years, until its formal description in 1997.

Caladenia lyallii

One to 4 flowers of 2–3 cm diameter grow on a 5–20 cm long, hairy, upright stem with, at the base, a single long leaf up to 1 cm wide. The flowers are white or pinkish, the petals and sepals wider than on the other New Zealand caladenias, the dorsal sepal often tinged brown-pink and arched over the column and labellum. The labellum may be striped red and white, and carries

Caladenia lyallii. IStG

4 regular rows of calli. The leaf is wider than those of the *C. carnea* complex and may be 1 cm wide.

There is some difference of opinion about the Australian and New Zealand forms of *Caladenia lyallii* and *C. alpina*. The Australian taxonomist David Jones separated the two on the basis of labellum structure, but New Zealand plants do appear to fall into 3 subgroups — a large Otago form apparently identical with the Australian *C. alpina*, a smaller Otago form, apparently identical with a larger central North  Island form and likely to be *C. lyallii*, and a third, small form from under pines at Iwitahi, which is either a local habitat-induced aberration or an undescribed taxon.

New Zealand's first collection of *C. lyallii* was from Otago, by Dr David Lyall, surgeon on the *Acheron*. The species is reasonably common, and the plant can be found under manuka and light scrub, to sea level in the south. It flowers from November to January and is predominantly insect-pollinated.

Bernard Cracroft Aston, Secretary of the Dunedin Naturalists' Field Club, minuted an excursion to Flagstaff on 7 November 1894:

> On reaching the open at the top of the hill the rain had steadily set in & most of us decided to return. Before doing so we collected . . . *Caladenia Lyallii*.

Caladenia minor

• Three Kings

This species is smaller than *C.* aff. *carnea*, its flowers usually solitary, and its sepals greenish on the outside, the other segments pink or white. The labellum midlobe is small, triangular without marginal calli, and pokes straight out. It grows in scrub and open places in forest, and flowers from October to January. It has been known as *C. carnea* var. *minor*. The name comes from J.D. Hooker, who wrote in his *Flora of New Zealand* of 1853: 'The smallest New Zealand

Caladenia minor. IStG

Caladenia nothofageti. IStG

species, 4–6 inches high, very slender, one-flowered, covered with spreading glandular patent hairs.' The accompanying illustration shows a flower with a labellar midlobe carrying marginal calli to its tip!

Caladenia nothofageti

This is a small plant similar to *C. chlorostyla*, but the flower lacks any stripes or spots and is white, often with a plain yellowish tinge, and usually grows in association with beech (*Nothofagus*) species. The labellar midlobe is long and bears long marginal calli. The labellar calli are also long-stalked. It was described formally for the first time in 1997.

CALEANA

A small Australian genus of 2 species.

Caleana minor

This occasional trans-Tasman vagrant grows up to 15 cm high, with a single linear leaf, and 1–7 flowers between October and January. The labellum is attached by an irritable claw, which flips it over when an insect alights on it. In profile the open flower has an uncanny resemblance to a flying duck. The species has been recorded from Kaitaia 1898–1912; Rotorua and Waiotapu 1891–1924, and after an interval, in Rotorua 1982 to the present. R.H. Matthews sent specimens to Cheeseman in 1898, writing: 'I cannot resist the temptation of sending a small orchid for identification. So far have found only 3 specimens,' but later, in 1912, after Cheeseman had identified the orchid, '*Caleana* plants are plentiful.'

Caleana minor: a South Australian plant. RB

CALOCHILUS

An Australian genus of terrestrial orchids, a few of which have spread to Papua New Guinea, New Caledonia and New Zealand. Most have hairy labella and are known as 'beardies'. Otherwise the plants are similar to *Thelymitra*.

Calochilus herbaceus

A plant with greenish yellow petals and sepals with heavy red-striped markings was rediscovered in the far north a few years ago and identified by Brian Molloy as the trans-Tasman vagrant *C. herbaceus*. In some plants the flowers lack the red pigment and are greenish white. The labellum tip is short, flat, bare and ribbon-shaped, the disc covered in long, thin, hair-like calli, the base metallic blue. There are prominent 'eyes' at the bases of the column-wings. The stem and leaf are blue-green, and the plant may reach 60 cm. It flowers from October to December.

This taxon was thought to be *C. campestris*, which in turn was thought to be extinct in New Zealand, until Doug McCrae rediscovered the plant in the Far North in 1987. It has been found only in Northland.

Calochilus herbaceus. IStG
Opposite: *Calochilus paludosus*. IStG

Calochilus paludosus

This plant is tall (up to 50 cm), with a very narrow fleshy leaf. Except for the red-brown beard on the labellum, which is twice the length of the rest of the flower and has a long, bare, strap-shaped tip, its flower parts are greenish, the petals and sepals often reflexed back almost against the ovary when fully open. There are no 'eyes' at the bases of the column-wings. It likes damp or even swampy areas, and flowers from October to December.

The early botanists found the different *Calochilus* taxa hard to identify. Henry Hammersby Travers found this species near Collingwood in 1881;

Calochilus robertsonii. YC

specimens were sent by John Buchanan to Baron von Mueller in Australia, the latter responding:

> I took immediate notice that this *Calochilus* might be identical with *C. paludosus* as you suggest . . . I must confess I am not clear about positive distinction between *C. campestris*, *C. robertsoni*, and *C. paludosus*.

Calochilus robertsonii

The leaf of *C. robertsonii* is wider than that of *C. paludosus*, and the flower does not open as widely. The colouring is similar, with prominent reddish stripes on the petals and sepals, and a hairy red beard-like labellum. The tip of the labellum is strap-shaped, short and twisted. There are prominent 'eyes' at the bases of the column-wings. It grows in open, sunny places, often in very dry and bare areas under eucalyptus. It flowers from November to December.

Thomas Kirk wrote in 1891 that he obtained good specimens (which he thought were *C. campestris*) from Rotorua 'through the kind exertions of my old friend the Rev. F.H. Spencer, who, although on the eve of leaving for England, gave himself considerable trouble in searching for this plant, and was rewarded with success.'

CHILOGLOTTIS

Of several Australian species of *Chiloglottis* (there have been a number of recent additions), 3 have been reported in New Zealand. One is self-pollinating and is one of New Zealand's most common orchids; the others, like all Australian species, have specific pollinators, and as these are absent from New Zealand the plants fail to thrive. They are terrestrials, which usually have a single hairless flower. The dorsal sepal is uppermost, the lateral sepals and petals narrow, the winged column more or less erect, and the labellum is attached by a short column-foot. They have 2 leaves and ovoid tubers.

Chiloglottis cornuta

- Chatham
- Antipodes
- Auckland Is.

This orchid is common, except in the north, by any forest track. It usually has 2 equal green leaves that lie close to the ground; 3–10 cm long, they are oval, veined, pointed and smooth. The green flower is 1–2 cm across. The dorsal sepal is oval, narrowing to its base, overtopping the column. The sepals and petals are narrow and pointed, the former curling down below the labellum, the latter more or less horizontal. The labellum is decorated with prominent green or brown calli in a range of patterns, perhaps signifying different taxa. The stem elongates greatly in fruit.

C. cornuta has adapted itself to our new forests; it grows happily in the mix of needles and bark beneath exotic pines and may be spread in the pine chips used in garden mulch. Flowering is from October to February, and it is predominantly self-pollinating.

G.M. Thomson of Dunedin wrote in 1878:

> The arrangement of the parts is so simple that an insect alighting on the labellum and advancing its head into the base could hardly fail to remove the pollinia; nor could one entering with pollen on its head fail to leave them on the stigma . . . I am inclined to think self-fertilization takes place in flowers which have not been visited by

Opposite, above: *Chiloglottis cornuta*; below, *Chiloglottis valida*. IStG

insects... I examined one sunny day twenty-two flowers growing in the open; of these only three had both pollinia removed...

Chiloglottis formicifera

This is a trans-Tasman vagrant, which has not been seen in the wild in New Zealand for 80 years. Unlike *C. cornuta*, the flower is borne on a prominent stalk about 80 mm high, and the margins of the leaves are distinctly wavy. Its Australian pollinator is absent from New Zealand, hence its failure to spread. At its one recorded site in New Zealand, Kaitaia 1900–15, it flowered in September.

Chiloglottis formicifera. GF

R.H. Matthews wrote to Cheeseman in 1900:

> The flower is very delicate and curious, quite new to me. Stem and petals kind of pinkish red, column pale green, labellum palest pink with narrow margins of dark shading, tubercles glossy black near the throat, shading off to reddish or lighter black towards the outer margins where the tubercles are smaller.

Chiloglottis valida

This trans-Tasman vagrant was first discovered in 1981 near Hanmer and in the Richmond Ranges in Marlborough. It was at first mistaken for *C. gunnii* but was eventually described as the new species *C. valida*. The plants are more robust than those of *C. cornuta*, with wider, longer leaves on a longer stem. The flowers are brown-purple. In New Zealand clones, the labellum has a stalked callus at the base and a sessile callus on the disc, with pairs of glossy black, ant-like calli on either side. It has been found more recently in exotic pine forests at 2 separate sites near Iwitahi. It flowers in December but spreads only vegetatively, since its pollinator does not live here. Thus its presence at several separate sites suggests a number of independent introductions.

CORYBAS

There are over a hundred *Corybas* species from southeast Asia to New Zealand. All are terrestrials with solitary (exceptionally double) flowers; the dorsal sepal is uppermost and is close to the tubular labellum; the column is short and leans backwards, with a discoid stigma. The petals and sepals of several species are long and thin, giving the plants a spider-like appearance. The tubers are spherical. The single leaf is flat, broad and more or less round, often silver-backed. The stem elongates greatly in seed.

None of the New Zealand species is now thought to be shared with Australia, though several of the 'helmet orchids' (those lacking the elongated sepals and petals of our 'spider orchids') are very closely related to Australian species.

Corybas acuminatus

C. acuminatus has a thin, veined, triangular leaf with a rippled edge; the flower is almost transparent, its dorsal sepal greatly elongated to make a fifth 'leg' for the spider, and its labellum flattened against the ovary. An orchid of shady damp forest, it is uncommon in the south, but densely packed colonies are easily found in the North Island, and at Waikaremoana and in the Hunuas it is the dominant forest floor *Corybas*. It flowers from September to December, and is predominantly insect-pollinated.

Corybas acuminatus. IStG

C. acuminatus was for most of this century misnamed *C. rivularis*. Mark Clements recognised the error, and he and Dan Hatch formally described this species as *C. acuminatus* in 1985. References to *C. rivularis* between 1906 and 1985 mostly refer to *C. acuminatus*.

Corybas carsei

This is New Zealand's rarest endemic orchid, if it is indeed different from the Australian *C. fordhamii*. It has at times been confused with *C. unguiculatus*.

The lateral sepals and petals are shorter than the labellum; the tip of the dorsal sepal is deeply cleft, and the labellar calli are confined to swollen tissue close to the apex and along the raised midline. It is confined to bogs, and as agricultural progress demands drainage of the surrounding grassland with consequent drying of the swamps, and as remnant swamps become infested with alien weeds, its habitat shrinks and it disappears. Burning the bogs is being trialled as a conservation measure. It is now known from only one spot in a swamp in the lower Waikato, where it flowers in September.

Dan Hatch notes that *C. Carsei* was named for Harry Carse, who with Henry Blencoe Matthews discovered the species in the Lake Tongonge bog near Kaitaia in 1910. The orchid has long since gone from Lake Tongonge. The draining of the lake in 1912 didn't immediately extinguish the species (there are Matthews specimens in Kew dated 1919 and marked 'very rare') but undoubtedly hastened the drying out of the bog. The main cause of the

Corybas carsei. EDH

plant's disappearance from Kaitaia would seem to have been over-collecting — there are a great many specimens in the various herbaria; one sheet alone of Matthews' displays 21 flowering plants!

Corybas cheesemanii

This is a tiny plant, the dorsal sepal a little maroon dome pushing up through the leaf-litter. Its lateral sepals and petals are short, often tiny hair-like vestiges. White-flowered forms have been recorded. The labellum has 2 closed conical spurs at the base. The leaf is 7 mm in diameter, round and pointed. The species prefers deep forest floor litter, manuka, taraire and beech, and is often almost buried. It flowers May–August.

Thomas Kirk named this species for Thomas Cheeseman, curator of the Auckland Museum for 50 years, after finding it at Blockhouse Bay in West Auckland in 1865. He wrote:

> I obtained a few imperfect specimens of this interesting plant from the Whau district about five years ago, but it was not in a fit state to allow of a diagnosis being drawn. Mr. Cheeseman subsequently found it in some quantity, and has kindly favoured me with good specimens and valuable notes . . .

It was for a time included in the related Australian *C. aconitiflorus*.

Corybas cheesemanii. ES

Corybas cryptanthus

• Three Kings

This is a curious, leafless orchid, which lacks chlorophyll. It is usually found growing with mosses, almost entirely beneath the manuka or beech litter of the forest floor. The flower is nearly colourless, but may be flecked with red and brown. The labellum is wide and fringed, the dorsal sepal as long as the labellum, the sepals and petals long and often emerging above the surface of the leaf litter. The bud emerges from a vestigial leaf bract. There is a long, horizontal, branching, thread-like, 1 mm diameter rhizome, with tuberous nodules and tiny bracts along its length. As with all *Corybas*, its red-flecked stems elongate (up to 15 cm) in seed. November, when leafless

Corybas cryptanthus. IStG

seeding stems can be found above ground level, is the best time for locating it.

This rare species flowers in July to September and is self-pollinating. The only reference to its having been seen south of Reefton and North Canterbury is an isolated report from Manapouri. It was described from material collected in the Dome Valley north of Warkworth by Bruce Irwin and Owen Gibson in October 1949 and supplemented by Dan Hatch. The plant had been gathered on several occasions as far back as 1880, but was never properly understood or described. R.H. Matthews, for instance, made several references in his correspondence with Cheeseman: '*Corysanthes* species, leafless, in fruit. NB you thought this might be *C. triloba*, or something new.'

Corybas dienemus

This species, described only from Macquarie Island, appears to be similar to *C. orbiculatus* in having short tepals, but is smaller and more upright.

Corybas iridescens

The leaf of this species is usually obviously stalked and is often blotched purple on its upper surface. The flower is large, dark red almost to black, lighter and brownish in Otago. The dorsal sepal is tawny to greenish with raised purple streaks darkening with maturity. The labellum is very sharply deflexed, flaring widely; it carries a bead-like callus at the entrance to the column cavity. It flowers from August to October. In Otago the leaf emerges from the ground in spring as a tight cone, which widens to reveal the immature flower, its petals and sepals curled above the other parts. As the flower matures, the leaf flattens and the sepals and petals straighten. It likes wet areas, and can often be found in running water. It is fairly common, flowering September to November, and is predominantly insect-pollinated.

G.M. Thomson noted in his diary (now in the Hocken Library) in 1879:

Corysanthes: the species found on stones in Nicholl's creek — now fast disappearing — may be either *C. rivularis* or *C. macrantha*. Like so many other plants they probably run into one another.

This was *Corybas iridescens* (it has not yet disappeared from the environs of Nicholls Creek in the Leith Valley near Dunedin), and his difficulty in separating it from *C. macranthus* indicates that he understood the similarity (both species have round leaves), and was not, as the northern botanists were, confused with what we now know as *C. acuminatus*.

Corybas iridescens. YC

Corybas macranthus

C. macranthus is the largest of the genus in New Zealand, liking well-lit sites, often under scrub, and forming large, loose colonies of many plants.

The stalked green leaf is thick and fleshy, silver-backed, often bearing brownish markings along the edge; the petals are shorter than the sepals (both are much elongated), the labellum dark reddish black, the whole flower 1.5 cm across. The northern form has a tawny patch in the centre of the purple-brown labellum and a tawny dorsal sepal. It only grows in shade and always has the flower below the leaf. The southern form has an all-dark labellum and dorsal sepal. The flower is usually borne above the leaf in exposed sites. It is common throughout New Zealand and flowers from October to January; it is predominantly insect-pollinated.

G.M. Thomson wrote in 1878:

> I could not understand why spiders frequented these flowers so much, but I soon found a sufficient cause. The only insects capable of removing pollen which were found about the flowers were small Diptera — probably a species of *Culex*. In several cases these small flies had penetrated into the tube of the flower, and, in their eagerness after the sweet juices found there, brought their heads into contact with both rostellum and stigma, and partly owing to the viscidity of these parts, and partly to the narrowness and bending of the tube, were unable to withdraw backwards. In some flowers insects were thus found still alive, in others they were dead, while in many others only portions of them, such as legs, wings, etc., were left, the spiders having devoured the rest.

• Chatham
• Campbell

Corybas macranthus. YC

Corybas oblongus

• Three Kings
• Chatham
• Auckland Is.

C. oblongus has a thin, oval, brown-veined, pointed, stalkless leaf and a tiny 5 mm diameter flower, its tubular, dark maroon labellum fringed with coarse pale teeth. Often there is a 'fence' or cluster of dark calli inside the base of the labellum. Robust plants may sprout a second flower in lieu of the fertile bract. It is uncommon in the south of the South Island, where it flowers from October to December (earlier further north); it is predominantly self-pollinating. White-flowered forms have been recorded. There appear to be consistent differences between two forms of this.

J.D. Hooker called the New Zealand spider orchids *Nematoceras*, but recognised later that they were similar to the Australian *Corysanthes*. Both were eventually included in *Corybas*. Of *N. oblonga* he wrote, 'Lip 1/5 inch, broadly reniform, cordate when spread out, deep blood-red purple, with transparent edges, margin in front sharply toothed . . .'

Corybas oblongus. IStG, ES

Corybas orbiculatus

The flower is in some ways similar to that of *C. rivularis*, and its rediscoverer, Bruce Irwin, at first included it in a group of several taxa with affinities to this species. The major difference is that the sepals and petals are very much shorter, only a little longer than the labellum. The labellum disc is broad and dark red, the margins inrolled to produce a narrow-pointed appearance. It flowers August to October.

C. orbiculatus is uncommon, growing in constantly wet sites, and appears to be predominantly insect-pollinated. This is not the taxon named *C. orbiculatus* in *Flora II*, but is the one that has been known as *C.* 'short tepals'.

Ernie Corbett and Bruce Irwin saw this plant in about 1950 near Wanganui: the New Zealand Native Orchid Group's *Newsletter* published Bruce's drawing in 1988. In 1989 he again reported finding what he called '*Corybas* C' in Taranaki. Brian Molloy recognised that Colenso's original collection of *C. orbiculatus* from near Mt Cook was in fact this taxon, not that referred to in *Flora II*. Plants called *C. orbiculatus* between 1970 and 1994 are likely to be *C. rivularis* or those with affinities to it.

Corybas orbiculatus. IStG

Corybas papa

The leaf is unstalked, i.e. strictly sessile. The flower is predominantly green, the labellum is compressed front to rear, its apex rounded, but with an inconspicuous apiculus. The petals project forward and outward. *C. papa* flowers from August to September. It grows on seeping road banks.

This taxon was included by Irwin in the *C.* aff. *rivularis* group as *C.* 'Mt Messenger' and was formally described by Molloy and Irwin in 1996.

Corybas rivularis

The flower is small with a narrow red labellum, the outer flexure of which is barely evident so that the apex projects forward well clear of the ovary. The labellum apex is tapering, as compared with *C. iridescens* and *C. macranthus*. The petals are nearly as long as the lateral sepals; the labellum and dorsal sepal are green, with or without red markings. The leaf is near orbicular, apiculate, often with a row of dark blotches near the margin. The orchid forms large colonies in wet places — stream banks, cliff face seepages, in the spray zone of waterfalls.

The plant was discovered by Allan Cunningham on 6 November 1826 in a gorge near Whangaroa (and later behind the Rainbow Falls on the Kerikeri River), and named by him *Acianthus rivularis*. Owing to a series of mistakes the plant was later confused with *C. orbiculatus* and *C. rotundifolius* (and even named as a distinct variety, *Corysanthes rotundifolia* var. *pandurata*) until in 1983 Clements found Cunningham's type material at Kew. The name *C. rivularis* is now applied to the plant previously tagged by Irwin as *C.* 'Kerikeri' and confirmed only from Kerikeri (and a couple of nearby sites) and New Plymouth.

Corybas rivularis. EDH

Opposite: *Corybas papa.* ES

Of the several taxa included by Irwin at one time or another in the *Corybas rivularis* complex, a number have already been accorded specific status; they are *C. papa*, *C. iridescens*, *C. orbiculatus* and *C. rivularis* itself. Several more taxa appear to be distinct, and are by now well known by their tag-names (*Corybas* 'rest area', 'whiskers', 'Kaimai' and 'Waiouru').

Corybas macranthus var. *longipetalus*. Although this taxon has been formally described as *C. macranthus* var. *longipetalus*, it is one of the *C. rivularis* complex, and has been tag-named *C.* 'Waiouru'. It has a short-stalked leaf as in *C. iridescens*, and though the flower resembles *C. papa* in shape it differs in that the petals project forward. The labellum may vary from green, lightly marked red to almost totally red. It flowers July to October, as far south as southern Wairarapa and northwest Nelson.

Corybas 'rest area'. The colour pattern closely resembles that of *C. papa*. This taxon differs from the other New Zealand *Corybas* species in that its dorsal sepal in robust plants arches upwards. Plants under stress and juveniles have it horizontal and can be confused with *C. papa*. The tapered tip does not clamp down over the labellum but arches upward above it. The tapered tip of the labellum barely reaches down to auricle level. It flowers in October in mossy swamps south of Taupo.

Corybas 'whiskers'. The colour usually resembles that of *C. papa* but the labellum is not compressed front to rear, and its inner surface is covered with minute pale hairs which obscure the pattern of veins. A maroon form is sometimes found. The auricles are particularly large and open forward. It flowers September to October.

Corybas 'Kaimai'. The flower is usually green, lightly marked dull red. The labellum tapers to an acute apex and the inner flexure is very sharply deflexed (about 130°). It flowers September to November.

Corybas 'rest area'. ES

Corybas 'Waiouru'. ES

Corybas 'whiskers'. ES

Corybas 'Kaimai'. ES

Corybas rotundifolius

This plant is similar to *C. carsei* but larger, never grows in bogs, and lacks the cleft tip to the dorsal sepal. Inward-facing calli are arranged along the raised labellum midline, short near the apex but much longer towards the column, and ceasing abruptly 3 mm from it. It is now confined to scrub and light forest between Warkworth and North Cape. Specimens in herbaria suggest that it once extended much further south. It flowers in July, whereas *C. carsei* follows in September–November.

Another misunderstood species, it was first collected by Colenso on 2 April 1846 near the village of Puehutai, on the upper Manawatu River. It was described by Hooker as *Nematoceras rotundifolia*. Unaware of the nature of Hooker's species, Cheeseman redescribed it from Kaitaia in 1899 as *Corysanthes matthewsii*; later it was included in the related Australian *C. unguiculatus*. In 1991 Colenso's *C. rotundifolius* was recognised as the same as Cheeseman's *C. matthewsii*.

Corybas rotundifolius. ES

Corybas trilobus agg.

C. trilobus is the most easily found *Corybas* everywhere except in the north. Its round, 3-lobed leaves form carpets of very large colonies in much of the bush, the tiny, solitary red and green flowers sitting spiderlike above or below the leaf. The dorsal sepal is rounded, the petals about a third the length of the lateral sepals. The leaf is usually wider than long, a constriction near the tip producing a 3-lobed effect, but it is very variable in leaf and flower.

• Chatham
• Campbell

There is almost certainly more than one taxon in what we know as *C. trilobus*. Beech forest plants begin to flower in July, their red-green flowers always above the leaf (near Queenstown the ground is still stiff with frost

Corybas trilobus. IStG

NEW ZEALAND NATIVE ORCHIDS 77

when they emerge). Other forms are larger, and the colours vary from ruby-red to white, and flower October to December. Populations north of the Bombays flower in June–July and have flowers below the leaf. A number of *Corybas* with trilobate leaves show differences in flowering time, size, and sometimes structure. (I have tagged two of these *Corybas* 'Rimutaka' and *Corybas* 'Trotters'.)

In several places rather curious forms of *Corybas* have been found, with characteristics somewhere between *C. trilobus* and either *C. macranthus* or members of the *C. rivularis* complex.

Common in most areas of bush, *C. trilobus* flowers then spreads vegetatively, so that large patches of leaves may show few flowers. It is predominantly insect-pollinated.

Corybas 'Rimutaka'. This undescribed taxon is dark red-black. It has affinities with *C. trilobus*, the flowers sometimes below and sometimes above the leaf, the dorsal sepal ridged and its tip sharp, the flower oval from the front, the long axis of the oval vertical. It flowers in October, and I have seen it only in Rimutaka State Forest Park.

Corybas 'Trotters'. This is a large undescribed taxon, dark red-black and late-flowering. It has affinities with *C. trilobus*, the flowers below, and their long lateral sepals appearing above, the layer of petiolate leaves. The leaves are as long as they are wide and may be 5cm across. It flowers October–December. Helen Dalrymple beckoned in 1937:

> Come with us in imagination, on an excursion up Stony Hill on a shiny summer morning . . . It is not long before we find our first spider orchids at the foot of some low manuka scrub . . . lovely dark ruby red flowers, one flower to a leaf, with rounded hoods, and long spider-like feelers . . . Shrieks of delight from other groups are heard as they discover fresh patches . . .

Corybas 'round leaf'. The flower is carried above a round petiolate leaf resembling that of *C. macranthus*. The dark red labellum is typical of *C. trilobus*, but the dorsal sepal is often tapered in the manner of *C. rivularis* and projects well beyond the labellum. So far found only beside small waterfalls near Ruapehu, it flowers October–November.

Corybas 'Rimutaka'. IStG   *Corybas* 'Trotters'. IStG

Corybas 'round leaf'. ES

CRYPTOSTYLIS

About 20 species of *Cryptostylis* are scattered through southeast Asia and Australasia, evergreen terrestrials with tough leaves and spreading, fleshy roots. The flowers are inverted, the large labellum uppermost.

Cryptostylis subulata

This Australian grows only in the swamps and bogs of Northland, where it is now well established. The tall flower spike of up to 20 flowers is supported by the surrounding rushes and sedges. The labellum is uppermost, oblong, up to 5 cm long and reddish yellow; the other segments are narrow. ('The labellum undoubtedly prettier than the other segments,' wrote de la Billardiere in 1806.) It flowers from December to January.

Cryptostylis subulata. IStG

CYRTOSTYLIS

An Australasian genus similar to *Acianthus,* small terrestrials with a single broad basal leaf and a thin upright stem bearing a few small flowers.

Cyrtostylis oblonga and *Cyrtostylis reniformis*

These 2 species are structurally similar except for the shape of the leaves — oblong and kidney-shaped, respectively — although the shape varies considerably anyway. They apparently do have different chromosome counts. The leaf is sessile, low on the stem, the flowers colourless to red brown with a flat, oblong, glistening, conspicuous labellum bearing 2 basal calli. They grow in scrub and light forest, or in the open, and flower in July to October.

In 1853 Hooker described the genus in his wonderfully compressed prose:

> A very small genus of delicate, green, herbaceous Australian, Tasmanian and New Zealand plants, with tuberous roots, slender stems, solitary, broad, cordate leaves, and few-flowered racemes of expanded somewhat two-lipped greenish flowers.

Cyrtostylis oblonga. IStG

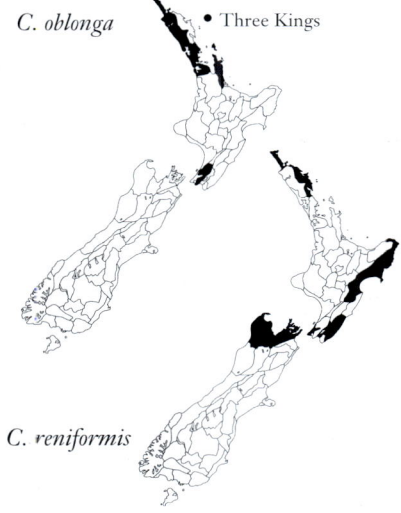

C. oblonga • Three Kings

C. reniformis

DANHATCHIA

An endemic New Zealand genus of one species.

Danhatchia australis

A rhizomatous, leafless epiparasite, associated with nikau and/or taraire, and lacking chlorophyll, although occasional chloroplasts in the cells of the leaf-bracts suggest that the species has evolved from a normal green-leaved plant. The stems are pinkish to dark brown, with several colourless leaf-bracts. It flowers from December to February; the flowers rarely open, and then only briefly. The sepals and petals have conspicuous cream-coloured tips.

The plant was initially thought to be a species of the Japanese genus *Yoania* but is now recognised as a monospecific New Zealand genus. Hatch's first specimen was collected by E. Kulka from Waipoua River on 28 January 1955: 'A single dried specimen, plucked at ground level and a little past full bloom . . .'

Above and opposite: *Danhatchia australis*. ES

DRYMOANTHUS

This genus of 4 species was distinguished from the similar Australian *Sarcochilus* in 1943. They are small perching orchids, with flowers in branching racemes, sometimes showing the labellum uppermost, the petals and sepals similarly shaped, the labellum fleshy and cup-shaped, joined to a short column-foot. The column is short and cylindrical; there are 4 pollinia in 2 pairs, attached by a stipe to the disc of a prominent rostellum; the stigma is deeply concave.

The elongated seed capsules ripen slowly. Each seed is attached by an umbilical hair; empty seed capsules may remain to the following season. They resemble in miniature the elongated capsules of vanilla, also an orchid, originally from South America but now widely cultivated throughout the tropics. The rhizomes spread widely along the branches and trunks of host trees. The leaves are arranged in 2 rows on either side of the stem, and although they rise alternately, they appear opposite each other on the abbreviated stem.

Drymoanthus adversus. YC, ES

Drymoanthus adversus

This is an epiphyte, growing on the trunks of trees (over 50 host trees in the Waikato) and on rocks. It has always been rare in the southern South Island, though less so in Fiordland. One or two racemes bear 4 mm long green flowers which are usually deeply flecked with purple, and the labellum has thickenings at each side within its cup, often joining to form a transverse bar. The leaves are shiny and thick, oval to oblong, and pointed. The capsules appear large for the size of the plant. Flowering October to December, it is predominantly insect-pollinated.

Banks and Solander had collected 'Epidendrum adversum' from Opurangi in 1769, and J.D. Hooker described it in his *Flora Novae-zelandiae* 'A small genus of New Holland and Malayan epiphytical plants, of which one species inhabits New Zealand.' We now know there are 2 New Zealand species.

Drymoanthus flavus

I first saw this orchid on miro trees on Stewart Island, the plant a 5 cm rosette, with stiff, dull, green, speckled, oval, pointed leaves, the roots spreading widely on the smooth bark.

Old flower stems persist from previous years, and small seedlings accompany the parent plants. Several flowers are pendant on the stem, each flower minute, 5 mm across, yellow with few red markings. The petals and sepals are more or less equal, open, long and oval, the labellum cup-shaped but lacking the transverse ridge of *D. adversus*. Only a few fruits develop on each stem; they develop slowly, and do not open to spread seed until the following spring.

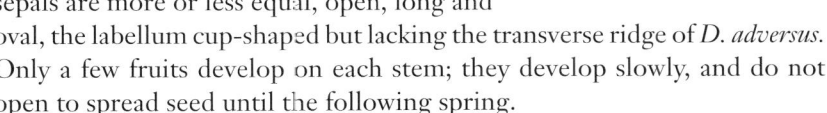

D. flavus is uncommon. It flowers from September to December and is predominantly insect-pollinated.

Among the Dunedin Naturalists' Field Club minutes for 1936, which are in the Hocken Library, is a report in Helen Dalrymple's handwriting of an outing to Leith Valley:

> Rare and beautiful native plants grow in profusion. Of these plants pride of place is given to the rarest, the epiphytic orchid *Sarcochilus adversus*, which in this favoured spot grows on three distinct host trees, the broadleaf and the yellow and white mapou or lemonwood ... The *Sarcochilus* was examined carefully, the bunchy tufts of purple spotted leaves, waxy blooms of yellowish green and withering whitish aerial roots adhering to the bark making a very quaint and interesting study.

This was *D. flavus*, and I saw a single plant on white mapou in the same place in 1990.

G.M. Thomson made the first record in September 1879: 'Johnstone brought to school today a species of *Sarcochilus* from Sawyers Bay, just coming into flower. This is the first time I have heard of this orchid in this part of the Colony.' By 1895 he would write, '*S. adversus* is becoming almost extinct in Dunedin.' The plant he referred to was *D. flavus*.

Drymoanthus flavus. IStG

EARINA

An endemic genus of 2 species (the similar taxa in New Caledonia, Tahiti, Samoa and Fiji are no longer regarded as *Earina*).

The earinas bear a number of racemes, each with several flowers which are small and hairless. The lateral petals and sepals are similar; the lobed labellum may be uppermost; the column is short and cylindrical with a terminal anther and 4 waxy pollinia; a deep stigma is separated from the anther by a prominent rostellum. The plant bears many cane-like, leafy, unbranched stems, more or less enclosed by leaf sheaths; it has long roots. The long thin leaves rise in alternate pairs, their blades twisted so that they face the same way.

Earina autumnalis

The heavily scented 'Easter orchid' (raupeka) flowers in autumn, when its fragrance may attract the searcher well before the plant is seen.

This is an epiphyte, but it will grow on rocks or even on the ground when trees fall or branches break, or when the orchid itself (less firmly attached than the other perching species) falls. The stem stands up if short, but grows to a drooping metre long; it is covered with stiff, 4–10 cm long, narrow, pointed, sometimes twisted leaves; it ends with the flower stem, turned upward if the stem is long and drooping. The flower stem carries many blooms, which are white and measure 0.5 cm across. These are classic orchids in miniature, with broad oval petals and sepals, and a broad, yellow-based labellum. *E. autumnalis* is a common orchid. It flowers on the previous year's spike from February to July, and is predominantly insect-pollinated. There are islands in Lake Manapouri that have *E. autumnalis* in hundreds growing as extensive mats in moss and liverwort carpets under the beech trees and out onto the lakeshore rocks; you can smell the scent well offshore.

In Dusky Sound J.R. Forster, naturalist on Cook's second voyage, wrote in his diary, 'After dinner I went ashore towards the watering place in our new Anchorage & found a very fine

Earina autumnalis. IStG

Epidendrum in flower, which spread a very agreeable smell.' It was *E. autumnalis*, drawn by George Forster on 29 March 1773. They could hardly have missed it for it is prolific along the shores of Dusky Sound.

An early *Otago Witness* reported:

> When pig-hunting in the Upper Waihera, we got on to a large boar that had given us a few hard runs on previous occasions,' Mr. W.O. Leith writes from Martinborough, Wairarapa. 'He went off on his usual route, with the dogs hard on his trail. His track took him around a long point. I set out for three-quarters of a mile over a fairly steep ridge, in order to get a passing shot at him. I found it very hard to get up the beech face, but reached the top, and I had started to go down through the undergrowth at a good pace when I ran into a bank of perfume. It was the sweetest and strongest perfume I ever smelt. I pulled up, and on climbing back a few yards, saw some flowers growing close to the ground. They were small, whitish, waxy flowers, clustered on hard, wiry stems. I thought at the time that they were the prettiest bush flowers I had seen. When I walked up to them the perfume seemed to change to a pungent smell, like the smell of large yellow garden bulbs. I took some of the flowers, crammed them into my hat, shoved my hat half through my belt, and continued the hunt until the dogs gave out. When I returned to my three mates, we sat down to have a smoke. I hardly had rolled a cigarette when one of them, about six feet away, sat up and asked where the sweet smell came from. I showed the flowers, which were strange to all my mates.

Opposite: *Earina autumnalis.* YC

Earina mucronata

The most common of New Zealand's perching orchids, 'peka-a-waka' is found on trees in many lowland forests, often in huge grassy-looking mats, covering well-lit branches and trunks. Each stem carries many tiny flowers on drooping clusters in spring (September to January).

The sometimes slightly fragrant flowers are creamy yellow, less than a centimetre across, with oval petals and sepals. The labellum is orange, broad and lobed at its base and outer end, with a narrow isthmus between. The leaves are slender and pointed, like stiff grass, with old dead flower stems sticking up untidily among them. The leaf-stems do not branch. The roots form a thick tangled mass attached to the tree bark.

E. mucronata is common and can be found in most open bush beside tracks. It flowers from October to December. It is predominantly insect-pollinated, as the prominent rostellum between the anther and stigma suggests.

John Lindley wrote in 1834:

> For fine specimens of this we are indebted to Mr. Cunningham who observed it 'growing commonly in moist woods upon the shores of the Bay of Islands, New Zealand, on mossy rocky banks, and on the limbs of trees, flowering in September and October, which in New Zealand is the season of spring.' From the latter circumstance we have contrived the generic name.

Sir William Hooker included *Earina* in a family of orchids he called Colensoanae, a tribute, alas, long forgotten.

In 1888 Georgina Hetley wrote:

> The roots of *Earina mucronata* often completely encase the branch on which it grows. The whole plant can be scaled off, when it forms a lovely object to hang up in a fernery, with its numerous heads of pale yellow flowers, hanging on their slender stalks, amongst the long, narrow, grass-like leaves.

Earina aestivalis was a name given by Cheeseman to a robust, short-columned, late-flowering coastal form of *E. mucronata*.

Opposite: *Earina mucronata*. RL

GASTRODIA

There are at least 5 New Zealand taxa in a genus ranging from the Himalayas to Japan and into southeast Asia and the Pacific. They are ground orchids with no chlorophyll and no leaves. The orchids gain their nourishment via a fungus that is parasitic on tree roots.

They bear a single raceme of several to many tubular flowers, the lateral sepals uppermost, the tube containing the oblong labellum which has wavy edges and bears longitudinal calli. The column may be short or long, bearing granular pollen and a basal stigma. The rhizome is bulky and full of starch; leaf vestiges are represented by scales on the stem and rhizome.

Gastrodia cunninghamii. IStG

Gastrodia cunninghamii. IStG

Gastrodia cunninghamii

G. cunninghamii is a tall plant, sometimes a metre in height and bearing up to 70 flowers on its one stem. The plant is brown, black or greenish, with only tiny scales on the stem as residual leaves. The flowers are knobby and tubular, formed by the fusion of the petals and sepals, which are separated only at their tips. The labellum is attached at the inside base of the tube so that only the black-tipped yellow end shows. The column is much shorter than the labellum, and folds down to place the pollen against the stigma.

G. cunninghamii nudges through the ground in spring like a brown asparagus shoot. It sometimes appears in association with introduced trees (*Pinus nigra* and rhododendrons), but in the wild it is found beneath open beech forest. It is common in the south, and flowers in December and January. It is predominantly self-pollinating.

William Colenso and Elsdon Best wrote of *gastrodia* tubers as one of the vegetable foods of the Maori (see introduction).

Gastrodia minor

G. minor is shorter than *G. cunninghamii* and has fewer (up to 10) flowers. Less than 30 cm tall, though usually only 15 cm or so, it is light brown overall, the thin tubular flowers containing the labellum and a much shorter column. It is common in some places in the north (under *Pinus nigra* at the Iwitahi Native Orchid Reserve for example), and is quite rare in the south. It flowers in December, and is self-pollinating.

Donald Petrie found it first under kanuka in Dunedin's town belt, and later at Opoho Creek. He wrote in 1892: 'I had the good fortune to find both plants *(Gastrodia cunninghamii* and *G. minor)* in flower in the neighbourhood of Dunedin at the same time, so that a very complete comparison of the two species was practicable.' By the turn of the century it had disappeared from these areas, 'choked out, in all likelihood by stronger and coarser aliens,' according to G.M. Thomson.

Gastrodia minor. IStG

Gastrodia 'long column'. IStG

Gastrodia 'long column'

Plants whose flowers have a long column similar to that of *G. sesamoides* and which have been at times mistaken for *G.* aff. *sesamoides* have been recorded for some years from different parts of New Zealand. These are often tall (80 cm), stout, light brown plants, the stem bearing 40 or so yellowish flowers. Some of these appear to be self-pollinating, their flowers at first dependant, later turning to point upward as they close, thus facilitating self-pollination. They flower in January. There appears to be more than one taxon, for one appears to be insect-pollinated with flowers smelling of freesias.

Gastrodia 'long column'. IStG

Hugh Wilson, who first recognised one of these undescribed taxa, wrote in his *Stewart Island Plants* (1982):

> These plants are more robust and densely flowered than *G. cunninghamii*; they also flower a month later. The long column inside the flower suggests an affinity with *G. sesamoides*, but this plant differs from that species in other respects and its relationships are not yet determined.

Gastrodia aff. *sesamoides*

Gastrodia aff. *sesamoides* is now regarded as different from the Australian species *Gastrodia sesamoides*. There seems to be variation (for example in the degree of tuberculateness of the flowers) even among New Zealand plants. The stem is up to 1 m tall, bearing 1–20 flowers, without or with few tubercles, varying from white through biscuit brown to dark mustard-yellow. The column is almost as long as the labellum. It flowers from October to December, and is not fussy about where it grows — it has been reported on traffic islands in Hamilton, Rotorua and Cambridge.

Donald Petrie wrote in 1893:

> This Australian orchid has not hitherto been recorded from New Zealand, but I am now able to add it to the species truly native to our Islands. I found it growing in considerable abundance in sparse scrub, At Kelly's Creek, Otira River, in January of the present year.

This could as easily have been *Gastrodia* 'long column' (see p.95).

Gastrodia aff. *sesamoides*. YC

GENOPLESIUM

These are the Australian midge orchids, small erect terrestrials with erect tubular leaves and many tiny inverted flowers borne on a thin stem.

Genoplesium nudum

Because the flower-spike breaks through the tubular leaf near its top, there is almost no leaf free of the flower-stem, hence the name. The flowers are dark red, with a dark red labellar callus divided by a linear depression. As with *G. pumilum*, the flowers are very long-lasting; they partly close when mature and can be confused with buds yet to open. *G. nudum* flowers from January to June.

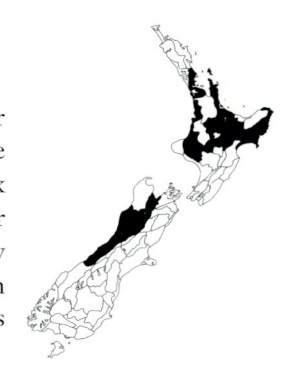

Genoplesium nudum. ES

Both *G. nudum* and *G. pumilum* were included in Hooker's 1853 *Flora Novae-zelandiae* as *Prasophyllum*, and remained thus until the old genus *Genoplesium* was reinstated in 1989.

Genoplesium pumilum

Here the free top of the leaf extends well into the flower-spike, although it seldom over-tops it. The flowers are creamy green, sometimes flushed pink with red markings, and open freely. The labellar callus shows several inconspicuous green ridges. *G. pumilum* favours poor scrub and mossy road banks. It flowers from March to June. A 40 cm plant in the far north needs further examination.

Genoplesium pumilum. ES, IStG

MICROTIS

A score or more species (there have been a number of recent additions from Australia) of 'onion orchids' range from southeast Asia to New Zealand, which probably has half a dozen taxa, 3 of which have been described.

Perhaps the least visually exciting of our native orchids, these are usually grassland plants with rather insignificant flowers. They are hairless, with a single raceme of many green flowers; the dorsal sepal is uppermost, forming a hood over the flower; the lateral sepals are of much the same length, the petals shorter. The labellum is oblong to triangular or oval, more or less hanging down, with calli at its base; the column is short with membranous wings ('little ears'), the anther terminal above an oval stigma; tuber ovoid; the single leaf more or less round in cross-section, and sheathing the stem for some distance.

Microtis arenaria

A short plant that grows up to 25 cm tall, with a flower similar to that of *M. unifolia*, but differing in the upturned pointed apex of its dorsal sepal, the prominently bilobed apex of the labellum with a decurved apiculum, and the long humped ovary. The whole plant has a characteristic yellowish tinge. The distribution is unknown: this Australian species was recognised from Northland only in 1995, where it was found flowering in November.

Microtis oligantha

M. oligantha has been found in damp turf or grassland, alpine meadow, flushed ground on open hillsides, and turfy lake shores. In comparison with *M. unifolia* it is small (often less than 5 cm tall), has fewer than 10 flowers, with a rounded dorsal sepal, a more regularly oblong labellum bearing large, squarish, rather flat basal calli, straight rather than curled

Microtis oligantha. IStG

Microtis arenaria. IStG

Microtis oligantha. ES

Microtis aff. *parviflora*. ES

Microtis unifolia. ES

lateral sepals, and column-wings that turn back, then forward. The flowers are green, but tend to whiten with age. It flowers from December to February and is predominantly self-pollinating.

Dan Hatch recognised that this was a new species for New Zealand in 1963:

> The most striking points of identification to the casual glance are the few (no more than 4 in the plants I have seen) loosely arranged flowers, the long slender pedicels and the large round dorsal sepals.

Microtis aff. *parviflora*

These plants are 10–30 cm tall, with many flowers crowded on the spike. The tip of the dorsal sepal is recurved. The labellum is more or less triangular, sticking out like a tongue, and though some have the smooth margins of the Australian *M. parviflora*, most do not, and probably represent a different undescribed taxon. Only the basal calli are obvious. A useful way to distinguish this from *M. unifolia* is that in *M.* aff. *parviflora* the column below the stigma is narrow, whereas in *M. unifolia* the column is as wide as the stigma. It grows in open places, flowering from October to January.

Microtis oblonga

This trans-Tasman species has been reported from New Zealand. It was included in *M. rara*, and is similar to *M. arenaria* and *M. unifolia*, but shows differences in the widely spaced, prominently stalked flowers, and the long (almost as long as the ovary, and pressed against it), narrow, oblong labellum; the labellar margins are similarly wavy and it has the same two basal calli and one apical callus.

Microtis unifolia agg.

The common onion orchid, as its generic name suggests, has minute flowers. The plant can be quite tall, but usually grows to less than 30 cm, fleshy stemmed with an onion-like leaf and many green flowers 3 mm in diameter.

You really have to look hard to recognise these as orchid flowers, but each does have the characteristic arched dorsal sepal (its tip pointed, compared with the blunt tip of the dorsal sepal of *M. oligantha*), petals beneath it, the lateral sepals curled to either side, and the broad, rough, irregular labellum below. Hundreds can be seen in the open, on clay banks, tussock grasslands, roadsides, sometimes in swampy sites: in any relatively unchanged damp pasture. It is predominantly self-pollinating, although small wasps have been reported pollinating flowers. Different habitats, flowering seasons and anatomy suggest that there must be several taxa currently included in *M. unifolia*.

J.R. Forster wrote in his diary at Queen Charlotte Sound on 13 November 1773, '. . . went over to Long-Island & mounted the hill, where we found several fine plants . . . We returned to dinner, having found a new Orch.' This was *M. unifolia*, described in 1786 by his son George Forster as *Ophrys unifolia*. It is thought to be very common, flowering from November to January, but true *M. unifolia* may prove to be less common than we now think.

Microtis unifolia. IStG

ORTHOCERAS

An Australasian genus of 2 closely allied species, one (or perhaps both) of which is found in New Zealand.

Orthoceras novae-zeelandiae

This species was regarded as identical with *O. strictum*, but Mark Clements separated the two in 1989, on the basis of chromosome differences and the shape of the labellum. Plants with both pointed and rounded labella certainly occur in New Zealand. These plants are up to 70 cm tall, with narrow, pointed, channelled leaves. They bear 2–12 flowers, the hooded dorsal sepal and long erect lateral sepals usually dark red, but sometimes green or yellow. The labellum has 3 lobes, and has a conspicuous yellow callus. The plants grow on clay banks and in open places, and flower from December to February. Achille Richard and Pierre-Adolphe Lesson described this plant in 1832; Lesson's original watercolour is in the museum at Rochefort in France.

Orthoceras novae-zeelandiae. YC, IStG

PRASOPHYLLUM

Mark Clements listed 81 Australian species (though the pygmy prasophyllums have since been reclassified as belonging to the genus *Genoplesium*, and there have been further Australian descriptions); there are more from New Caledonia.

New Zealand has 2 accepted taxa, although the anatomy of *P. colensoi* is variable, and it may be split into several species. They are ground orchids, hairless, with racemes of many flowers, the labellum uppermost. The dorsal sepal is often curved backward, the lateral sepals narrow, the petals shorter. The labellum is more or less trowel-shaped, the column short, stigma discoid, rostellum prominent, and tubers oval. The single leaf is tubular and sheathes the stem for a variable distance.

Prasophyllum colensoi

The 'leek orchid' is interesting in that its flowers appear 'upside down', the labellum uppermost. It ranges from quite red to the usual greenish-yellow.

Prasophyllum colensoi. IStG

The plant grows 15–30 cm high, an upright ground orchid bearing a solitary leaf, tubular and grooved, overtopping the flower. Several flowers are evenly spaced up the stem, each about 5 mm across. It is easily found in any open tussock or grassland, but is more common in the south, often in damp or sedge areas of swamps or swamp margins. Plants can be robust with crowded flowers, although smaller plants with fewer flowers occur. I have seen it at over 1000 m near Centre Pass on the Manapouri to Dusky Sound track. It flowers from October to January, and is predominantly self-pollinating.

G.M. Thomson noted in 1878:

> The flowers are somewhat sweet-scented, and though dull-coloured, are tolerably conspicuous, but there appears to be no trace of a nectary. Nor from the position of the parts is it very probable that an insect could remove the pollinia, so as to place the loose, incoherent grains on the stigma of another flower. The species is evidently well fitted for self-fertilization.

Prasophyllum aff. *patens*

Prasophyllum aff. *patens* was previously regarded as identical with the Australian *P. patens*, but is now regarded as an undescribed New Zealand taxon. These are tall plants of swamps and bogs, often growing in open water. The flowers may be yellow with a black or white labellum, or greenish red with a white labellum. The labellum is conspicuous, broad, with a wavy edge. The flowers open in December to February.

Cheeseman received specimens from Maungatapere (Harry Carse) and Great Barrier Island (Thomas Kirk), and he himself collected from the Ngaere Swamp in Taranaki. He wrote: 'Easily distinguished from *P. colensoi* by the much greater size, larger paler flowers, and longer lip, which has a much more conspicuous recurved lamina . . .' They have a strong, sweet fragrance, at least to those who can smell *Boronia*.

Opposite: *Prasophyllum* aff. *patens*. YC

PTEROSTYLIS

There are many greenhoods in Australia (Clements lists 100 species and several natural hybrids, and more have been described since); Papua New Guinea has a couple, New Caledonia has several and New Zealand has 25.

They are ground orchids whose flowers are green, often with red pointings, the dorsal sepal and petals forming a hood, the lateral sepals often joined together and pointed. The labellum is small and mobile, and with the column is mostly contained within a cylinder formed by the other segments of the flower; it sometimes has an appendage which has a frilled end. The column is long, with more or less oblong wings on each side of the rostellum; a terminal anther bears 4 crescentic pollinia.

The stigma is 2-lobed, elongated vertically, in the middle of the column. The tuber is ovoid. Several leaves may form a rosette at the base of the stem, or may be distributed up the stem; they are variously shaped but mostly long and thin. These plants trap insects, but they are not carnivorous. When the sensitive labellum of most species is touched by an insect it springs backward to form a narrow tube with the column. The trapped insect escapes through this tube, picking up the sticky pollinia for the next plant as it goes. The labellum can be triggered in a live flower by a light touch.

Pterostylis agathicola. IStG

Pterostylis agathicola

A narrow grass-leaved taxon, the 3–4 leaves usually spread out, but sometimes arched to horizontal. The labellum tip is unevenly constricted. Like *P. brumalis*, it has a mycorrhizal affinity with fungi that thrive in the litter of leaves, twigs, bark and cones that gather under kauri, and is never found out of the kauri zone. It flowers from August to September. This has been thought to be a variety of *P. graminea* and even of *P. montana*, but it is now regarded as a distinct entity.

Pterostylis alobula

Mature flowering plants are 15 cm tall and have sessile, bracteate leaves. The labellum is narrowed in its upper half, with a slightly swollen, truncate or crenulate tip. The sinus between the lateral sepals is more acute than,

Pterostylis alobula. YC

and lacks the protruding central lobe of, *P. brumalis* and *trullifolia*. It grows in scrub and light forest, and flowers from May to August. The juvenile plant is a rosette of stalked, trowel-shaped leaves; and adolescent forms have stalked, trowel-shaped leaves at the base and sessile bracteate leaves towards the top of the stem. This is the species from which Cheeseman made his famous observations on pollination, later quoted by Darwin in his book on orchid pollination.

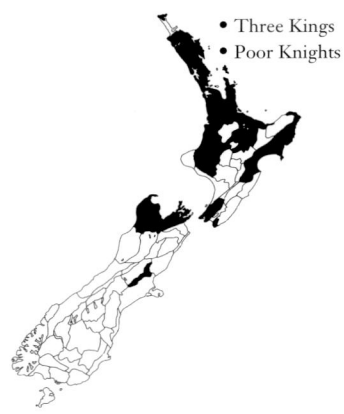

• Three Kings
• Poor Knights

Pterostylis areolata

An inhabitant of grassland and light scrub, this species is about 15 cm tall, with 2–4 green, rather broad, oval, membranous leaves, the uppermost smaller than the others, rarely overtopping the flower. The single green flower (which sometimes has red or dark brown tips to the caudae) has a dorsal sepal with its tip downturned, the lateral sepals rather short and often turned back and down. The petals are broad to their tips, and are shorter than the dorsal sepal. The labellum is elliptic and slightly arched; the column is as tall, with a long stigma.

Local and uncommon, *P. areolata* flowers from October to December, and is predominantly insect-pollinated. Petrie first described it in 1918 from specimens collected by Cockayne and Kirk in Marlborough and Canterbury.

Pterostylis australis

Many orchidologists doubt the existence of *P. australis* as a distinct species, and indeed, plants I have seen that fit the usual description in Fiordland grow in the same colonies as typical *P. banksii*. Others seem to merge with the undescribed southern taxa tagged *P.* aff. *montana*.

The species is described as 10–25 cm tall, with 4–5 leaves, shorter than

Pterostylis areolata. IStG

those of *P. banksii*, the shape changing from below upwards, the lowest elliptic, the uppermost grass-like, few of them overtopping the flower. The single flower has an elongated dorsal sepal (not as long as that of *P. banksii*), and lateral sepals that are greatly extended in their points, considerably overtopping the rest of the flower. Otherwise the description of column and labellum are as for *P. areolata*, although the stigma is described as long-oval, often as broad as the column, overlapped by the wings from above. It flowers from November to December, and is predominantly insect-pollinated.

J.D. Hooker wrote in his *Flora Novae-zelandiae* (1853) that *P. australis* was 'Nearly as large as *P. banksii*, but the leaves are shorter, broader, not keeled, reticulated.' In 1953, Owen Gibson, Dan Hatch and Bruce Irwin wrote that 'further investigation on the variability of the groups within the *P. australis-banksii* complex is required. Probably only one, polymorphic, group is present.' Lucy Moore, however, thought in 1970 that it was 'useful to retain the concept of *P. australis* for the very abundant and often very large Fiordland plant . . .' Everybody has a different idea of what *P. australis* really is.

Pterostylis banksii

P. banksii is a magnificent greenhood. Mostly green it may be, but it seems to embody the panache of orchids.

The plant grows to 30 cm tall, its 4–6 leaves long (up to 25 cm) and narrow. The flower itself can be 5 cm high, the long tips of the dorsal and lateral sepals often red in contrast to the green and white flower. The petals are much shorter than the dorsal sepal, the labellum and column of much the same height, and the stigma long, narrow and not very prominent. It is common, growing on sheltered banks and flowering from October to December. It is predominantly insect-pollinated (the forward-leaning column makes it unlikely that pollen will fall onto the rather flat stigma).

In 1826 Allan Cunningham found *P. banksii* on the bank of a stream in the Bay of Islands; it was over 30 cm tall. He described it as 'remarkable for the noble size of the flower', took some to Sydney and later sent them to Kew, by which time they had died back to tubers and were presumed dead. The next season, however, a perfect specimen emerged, flowered, and was painted by Francis Bauer; his painting appeared in Curtis's *Botanical Magazine* of 1832 (see page 15).

There is a distinct taxon, endemic to the Chatham Islands, known as *P. banksii* var. *silvicultrix*.

Opposite: above, *Pterostylis australis;* below, *Pterostylis banksii*. ES

Pterostylis brumalis. IStG

Pterostylis brumalis

As with *P. alobula*, plants have clear juvenile and adult forms, depending on tuber size (though there is no intermediate form). The stem-leaves of adult plants are relatively broad and tend to be bunched towards the top of the stem. The dorsal sepal is strongly curved in, with the petals held horizontally, while the sinus of the lateral sepals has a very prominent protruding lobe. The habitat, as with *P. agathicola*, is confined to the immediate vicinity of the kauri, apparently because of dependence on a mycorrhizal association with fungi that thrive in rotting kauri litter; *P. brumalis* flowers from April to July.

The species was confused with *P. trullifolia* until Hatch separated it in 1949; it was he who noted, 'Petals strongly incurved, horizontal to the dorsal sepal, producing a conspicuous "cobra-hood" effect'.

Pterostylis cardiostigma

The leaves are stiff and straight, like broad blades of grass, and stick out at an angle from the stem, giving the plant a characteristic spiky appearance. Flowerless plants, or plants in early bud, have been confused with *P. banksii*, but with familiarity even young plants can be positively identified. The flower is erect and tight, its petals and short sepals closely adjacent, with a heart-shaped stigma. The ovary has 6 orange ridges. It can be quite common in montane forest and in scrub under trees and scrub. It flowers in October and November.

Amazingly, plants of this species were thought to be young *P. banksii* until Dorothy Cooper recognised those at Days Bay in Wellington as something different, and described the new species in 1983; at that time the species was known only from the lower North Island, but since then the distribution has grown considerably.

Pterostylis cardiostigma. IStG

Pterostylis cernua

This 6–12 cm tall greenhood has narrow semi-nodding flowers with filiform free points to the lateral sepals. It has been collected from only one roadside site near Arthur's Pass, and was first described in 1997. It flowers November to January.

Pterostylis foliata

P. foliata is a tall, slender greenhood, up to 30 cm, the short oval leaves mostly crowded into a sort of rosette at the base, with a couple of longer and thinner leaves hugging the stem. The single flower is erect, about 2 cm tall, the dorsal sepal horizontal, the petals as long, and broad to their tips. The lateral sepals have erect, rather parallel tips overtopping the rest of the flower. The labellum is narrow and triangular, the column shorter, the stigma oval and prominent. Rare in most regions, it flowers in November and is self-pollinating.

Pterostylis foliata. IStG

Donald Petrie reported this species from Signal Hill, Milburn and Tuapeka Mouth in 1895. G.M. Thomson noted in his diaries, 'collected about Black Jack's Point and Signal Hill', and the *Otago Witness* reported that it had been seen on an outing of the Dunedin Naturalists' Field Club to 'Waterworks Creek' in 1894. I have seen it in none of these places, perhaps because, as the Field Club minutes of 1894 relate, 'A patch of *Pterostylis foliata* was run against and was eagerly collected.' Or perhaps because early reports wrongly identified the plant, for as the *Otago Witness* of 14 December 1895 reported of the Waterworks Creek specimens, 'This has since turned out to be *Chiloglottis cornuta*.'

Pterostylis graminea

P. graminea is a slender plant, the 4–6 grassy leaves keeled, narrow and erect, overtopping the flower. The flower is small, 1.5 cm tall, its dorsal sepal up or downcurved, the petals broad to their tips and a little shorter, the lateral sepals sharp-pointed and erect. Labellum and column are of about equal height, the stigma narrow. It grows in dark bush and scrub, by bush tracks all over the country. It flowers from August to December, and is predominantly insect-pollinated. There is such variation in shape and

Pterostylis graminea. IStG

flowering period among plants included in this name that it seems likely there are several taxa.

Helen Dalrymple wrote in 1937 that her Dunedin schoolgirls:

> ... finally discover two rather poor plants of *Pterostylis*, also under manuka, and not far from the Logan Point Quarry ... We know there must be far better specimens somewhere in the neighbourhood; but the morning is nearly over, and we scurry down by various breakneck routes to catch the 11.35 a.m. train ...

Pterostylis humilis

This is a plant of subalpine scrub. It usually has a rosette of three broad, pointed, bluish green leaves with parallel ribbing easily confused with those of *Chiloglottis cornuta*. The flower is erect, the sepals short, the laterals hardly exceeding the dorsal sepal. The tip of the labellum is constricted; the stigma is very large and globose. The stem elongates after flowering. It flowers in December and January. H.B. Matthews found plants at Ruapehu in 1921, took them home to Auckland, potted them up, and sent the inevitable stunted specimens to Australia to Dr Richard Rogers who described the species from these miserable things and from a photograph of the plant in its natural habitat.

Pterostylis irsoniana

The leaves are curved, and look like heavily keeled variegated (green/brown/white) blades of grass. The labellum is a long triangle, gradually narrowing to a slightly swollen, truncate or cucullate obtuse tip. This species is unique among *Pterostylis* in having a large, dark, prominent callus at the base, and sometimes smaller calli along the top midline. It grows in subalpine scrub, and flowers December–February.

Dan Hatch described the species in 1950, naming it 'to acknowledge the labours and enthusiasm of Messrs. J.B. Irwin and O.E. Gibson, who between them have done much to elucidate the orchid flora of Mount Egmont'.

Opposite: above, *Pterostylis humilis*. IStG; below: *Pterostylis irsoniana*. YC

Pterostylis irwinii. ES

Pterostylis irwinii

A large, slender-leaved *Pterostylis*, often with reddish tints. The flower is upright, slender and minutely hairy (especially at the junction of the lateral sepals); the labellum is evenly tapered. It flowers November to December, and until 1998 had been found in only one site near Ruapehu. It has now been found near Takaka.

Pterostylis micromega

The leaves of *P. micromega* often have an undulating margin; they are rarely arranged in a basal rosette, but are usually scattered up the stem. The flower is large for the size of the plant, and is pale green with broad white patches. The dorsal sepal is incurved and may be reddish; the lateral sepals do not diverge greatly. This is a plant of swamps and bogs, rarely growing in open water. It flowers from November to February. This is a rare species, and small numbers are now known from only a few swamps in the central North Island, northern Waikato and on the Chatham islands (and in northwest Nelson in 1998).

Pterostylis micromega. ES

Pterostylis montana

The true *P. montana* usually has an overall bronze colour with varying amounts of grey and red. The leaves are narrow and erect. The flower is squarish, with a rather blunt dorsal sepal and petals, and blunt, more or less flat tips to the lateral sepals, which are often curled forward and do not overtop the rest of the flower. The labellum is oblong, its tip very twisted to one side or the other, its midrib prominent, and longer than the column. The stigma is short and globular to heart-shaped, overlapping the column at the sides.

This is a common plant, which flowers from October to December and is predominantly self-pollinating; the upright flower with its rather prominent stigma readily 'catches' pollen falling from the anther.

In 1949 Dan Hatch commented on specimens collected by Cedric Smith from Halfmoon Bay on Stewart Island: 'Endemic — not uncommon about the *Nothofagus* forests on Mount Ruapehu; Lake Manapouri; abundant throughout Stewart Island.' Thomas Kirk had seen this plant on Stewart Island, and wrote in 1884: 'The dwarf variety of *Pterostylis banksii*, with abbreviated sepals, is common in open places in the forest.'

Pterostylis aff. *montana*. Several taxa are no doubt included under this catch-all name; all show some similarities to *P. montana* (though often more to *P. banksii*), but some are green rather than bronzed, and usually their flowers are larger, their lateral sepals longer and rolled into tubes (*cf* the flat lateral sepals of true *P. montana*). They have more spreading, arched leaves than *P. montana*, the flowers more slender with elongated dorsal sepal and petals, the lateral sepals tail-like and overtopping the rest of the flower. The labellum is oval, the midrib less prominent. The stigma is long and oval, and does not overlap the column at its sides. One taxon from the Catlins forests has been dubbed *P.* 'Catlins', and others from various North Island sites are as different from each other as each is different from *P. montana*.

Some taxa of *P.* aff. *montana* are very common. They flower from September to December, and appear to be predominantly insect-pollinated: a large upward-pointing rostellum keeps the pollinia separate from the rather flat stigma.

Helen Dalrymple wrote in 1937: 'For fine fat specimens of *Pterostylis* you could search the lower slopes of Flagstaff or wander up the alluring tracks of Trotter's Gorge.' This was one of the 2 very common Otago forms of *P.* aff. *montana*.

Pterostylis 'Catlins'. An undescribed but distinctive broad and arch-leaved *Pterostylis* with affinities to *P. montana*. The labellum is arched and tapering. It flowers in September.

Pterostylis nutans

The leaves of *P. nutans* grow in a rosette round the base of the stem, and have undulating margins. The flower 'nods' (hence the name), the ovary bent so that the flower faces downwards. There have been 3 confirmed records for New Zealand of this occasional trans-Tasman vagrant: Kaitaia 1910–1915, Castor Bay, on Auckland's North Shore, 1942, and Waihaha, west of Taupo, in 1995. Flowering at Waihaha has been in October, and the flowers do not set fruit, as its insect pollinator is not present in New Zealand.

Pterostylis montana. IStG

Pterostylis aff. *montana* from Otago. IStG

Pterostylis 'Catlins'. IStG

Pterostylis nutans. IStG

Pterostylis aff. *obtusa*. GD

Pterostylis aff. *obtusa*

Flowering plants resembling the Australian *P. obtusa* group were collected from near Nelson in 1998. Among New Zealand species they most resemble *P. trullifolia*, but have a shorter dorsal sepal, wider petals, a blunt labellum and a red-marked column. The juvenile rosettes have 2–3 large round leaves. They flower February to May on poor soil in manuka and gorse.

Pterostylis oliveri

This is a robust plant, often 30 cm tall, with a 5 cm flower. The wide leaves form a basal rosette or are scattered up the stem. The dorsal sepal is strongly curled downward and then often forward, the lateral sepals diverging at a narrow angle, with long more or less erect (or slightly backward-pointing) 'tails'. It is a plant of montane forest, flowering from November to January. It is the dominant greenhood from the Arthur's Pass area, and its distribution extends north to Golden Bay. Donald Petrie described it from specimens flowering in January at Kelly's Creek, Otira, in 1893, and dedicated it to: 'Professor D. Oliver, FRS, of Kew, in acknowledgement of valued assistance in my botanical studies.'

Opposite: *Pterostylis oliveri*. ES

Pterostylis paludosa. IStG

Pterostylis paludosa

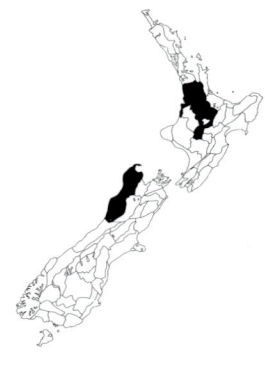

This is a pale green, grass-leaved species, the leaves short and upright, held close to the stem. The lateral sepals are short, barely exceeding the dorsal sepal. The tip of the black-keeled labellum is symmetrically constricted, occasionally twisted. The stigma is broadly heart-shaped. A slender plant of North and northern South Island transitional low moor to high moor bogs becoming dominated by wire-rush, *Empodisma minus*, it flowers from October to January.

Hatch found it in the swamps near Waiouru and, along with *P. micromega*, regarded it as a variety of *P. furcata* (var. *linearis*). Moore, from dried specimens, thought it indistinguishable from *P. montana*. Certainly it is similar to *P. montana*, but it is larger, the flower more slender, and it is pale green compared with the bronze green of *P. montana*.

Pterostylis patens

A robust grass-leaved plant of montane and subalpine forests, once thought to be a variety of *P. banksii*. The leaves are wide. The dorsal sepal is curved downward, but the most obvious characters are the strongly recurved 'tails' of the lateral sepals which often meet behind and below the ovary. It flowers December to January.

Colenso planted its tubers in a pot in 1883,

> . . . and they have grown strongly and flowered. I have had, however, but one fresh flower to examine, but this was so large, fully developed and gaping, that I had no difficulty in so doing, and that without breaking up or even gathering the specimen. Its form is striking, and its habit peculiar; all its floral parts being so very open and free, and its lateral sepals wholly deflexed horizontally; in all these characters I have not seen anything like it among all the flowers of the genus, nor in those of Australia and Tasmania.

Despite the strength of Colenso's conviction, Cheeseman included it in *P. banksii*, Hatch later re-elevating it to varietal rank. It is now again regarded as a distinct species.

Pterostylis patens. YC

Pterostylis porrecta. IStG

Pterostylis porrecta

A species of similar size to *P. graminea* but with arching leaves and lateral sepals that arch forward and downward away from the dorsal sepal; the labellum is tapered. It flowers in December. So far found only in 5 sites in southern Hawke's Bay, Eastern Wairarapa, Nelson and Marlborough.

Pterostylis puberula

This is a small plant, growing up to 10 cm. It has a basal rosette of trowel-shaped leaves on narrowly winged stalks, and hairs on the flower-stem. The dorsal sepal is very short and blunt. The lateral sepals have a high, rather shallow sinus with a small inflexed lobe, and long, erect 'tails' that are sometimes thickened at the tips. It flowers from September to December.

The Australian *P. nana* has been split into at least 20 different taxa, none of which appears to match the New Zealand *P. puberula*. It is known from small colonies in the Far North and near Thames, though there are old records from Mt Hikurangi and Wellington. Hooker described it in 1853 from plants collected from Auckland by Sinclair.

Pterostylis tanypoda

P. tanypoda has in the past been confused with *P. cycnocephala* but is now distinguished from that Australian species. It is a tiny (5–10cm tall) plant, with a basal rosette of oval leaves and a stout stem covered with sheathing leaves. Many of the specimens in herbaria labelled *P. mutica* are in fact *P. tanypoda*, and no doubt collectors have often confused them.

P. tanypoda has 1–7 flowers on the stem, striped blue-green and white, each up to a centimetre in height. The dorsal sepal and petals are broad and short, the lateral sepals joined almost to their tips to form a downward-pointing platform on which the labellum lies. The labellum is short and blunt, and at its rear end has a large appendage with a knob that juts forward. The column is short and wide, with broad hairy wings; the stigma is oblong. It is difficult to find, but it flowers, usually in grassland, from December to January. It is predominantly self-pollinating.

The Australian naturalist-artist Robert FitzGerald described *P. cycnocephala* in 1876 and, as Hatch wrote in 1953,

> ... was not quite sure in which taxonomic category the plant belonged, and was inclined to blame his indecision upon the lack of any definite taxonomic rules.

Pterostylis tanypoda. IStG

Pterostylis tasmanica. ES

Pterostylis tristis. VS

Pterostylis tasmanica

A 10 cm high plant with a basal rosette of leaves, though in mature flowering plants they may grow up the stem. The lateral sepals are deflexed. The characteristic feature is the thread-like labellum, which is covered with long yellow hairs and has a dark brown callus at the tip. It flowers in October. For years it has been confused with the similar Australian plants *P. barbata* and *P. plumosa*, but in 1994 *P. tasmanica* was recognised by David Jones as a distinct species, occurring in Victoria, Tasmania and New Zealand.

130 NEW ZEALAND NATIVE ORCHIDS

Pterostylis tristis

This is the species once thought to be the Australian *P. mutica*. It is also so similar to *P. tanypoda* (with its several small flowers) that it was often confused with that in the past. In contrast to *P. tanypoda*, the plant is often brownish, the labellum appendage has no forward-projecting knob, and it flowers from October to November. It is said to be predominantly self-pollinating, and grows in open grassland; it is difficult to find.

The Dunedin Naturalists' Field Club referred in 1882, in the short-lived *Journal of Science*, to '. . . the rare *Pterostylis aphylla*, Lindley, found by Mr. S. Fulton near Outram.' Cheeseman realised their mistake, and identified the plant as *P. mutica*.

Pterostylis trullifolia

This species is like a very slender (and often very tall) *P. alobula*, with the same three growth stages — juvenile rosettes, intermediate forms, and flower-bearing adults. It has, like *P. brumalis*, a pronounced protruding lobe in the sinus of the lateral sepals. A characteristic is that the veins of the juvenile rosette leaves stand out so the leaves appear embossed. It flowers from May to October. An unusual form has been recorded from Northland: the petals diverge from the dorsal sepal to form a trident shape. Early records of plants called *P. trullifolia* may refer to *P. alobula* or *P. brumalis*. The last two were separated off by Hatch as late as 1949 as varieties, and by Moore in 1969 as true species.

Pterostylis venosa

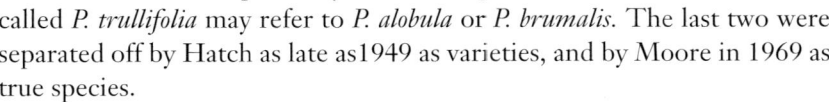

P. venosa is a small greenhood, a plant less than 10 cm in height, the leaves oval, broad, membranous, veined and partly hiding the stem. It grows in subalpine scrub and forest margins.

Pterostylis trullifolia. ES

The single, 15 mm tall flower is on a short stalk, often overtopped by the leaves: the dorsal sepal and petals short and blunt, the lateral sepals short and barely overtopping the flower. The labellum is narrow and triangular, arched and protruding, its inner surface in northern plants said to be covered with short, downward-pointing hairs. The stigma is narrow-elliptic. It is fairly common; it flowers in November or earlier, and is predominantly self-pollinating.

Colenso wrote in 1896:

> I have only received two specimens of this little plant... unfortunately, though whole and perfect, they have been pressed very much in drying, so that it has been a difficult matter to ascertain correctly their finer internal construction, on which so much depends, and I have only dissected one of them.

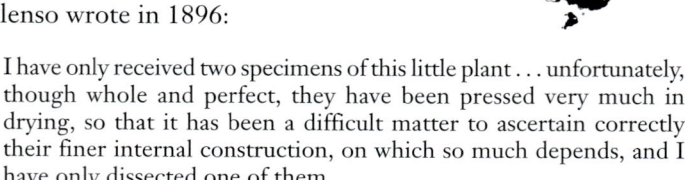

Opposite: *Pterostylis venosa.* ES

SPIRANTHES

Spiranthes is currently thought to have only one species in Australasia, although it is a worldwide genus of several hundred species.

Spiranthes sinensis

Although it can grow to a metre tall, New Zealand specimens of the 'ladies' tresses' orchid are seldom more than 30 cm. They are evergreen orchids of bogs and wet areas, with a cluster of swollen rhizomes. The stem is erect, much longer than the leaves, and bears many 5 mm flowers, more or less spirally arranged up the stem. The flower parts are arranged in a cylinder, usually dark pink except for the white labellum, although entirely white forms occur in the north. The labellum is broad and turned down at its

Spiranthes sinensis. IStG

fringed tip. The column is narrow, the stigma broad and prominent below the anther. There are half a dozen basal leaves, 5–10 cm long by 1 cm wide, with a few bracts up the stem.

S. sinensis which is rare in New Zealand, flowers from January to April. It is predominantly self-pollinating: the rostellum is almost invisible, and cannot keep the pollinia from contact with the subjacent stigma.

This is the most international of our species, and its type locality is China. The modern Chinese orchidologist S.C. Chen wrote that it was called 'ni', or 'fragrant ribbon-grass'. Colenso found it near Te Awamutu in 1842: 'Leaving the swamp and entering the plain beyond it, I discovered a new elegant plant of the Orchideae family and genus *Microtis*, possessing a beautiful carmine-coloured perianth . . .' He sent it to Hooker, who recognised it as *Spiranthes*.

Spiranthes sinensis IStG

THELYMITRA

A genus of over 50 species, most of them Australian, these are the most colourful of our ground orchids. They open on dry days (hence the common name 'sun orchids') and stay obstinately shut in damp weather.

They have single leaves, and stems bearing a raceme varying from one to many flowers. All have, at first glance, rather similar flowers and leaves. Sorting out the differences among the various species can be difficult; identification is usually made by comparing the structures of the columns.

The flowers are more regular in shape than those of other orchids, because the labellum and dorsal sepal are of much the same triangular form as the other petals and sepals. The column is short, its wings joined in front (at least partly hiding the anther) with various processes and decorations.

Thelymitra aemula. ES

The stigma is broad and flat. The single leaf is long and narrow, often quite fleshy, sheathing the stem at its base; smaller stem leaves appear further up. The tuber is oval.

Thelymitra aemula

The flowers of *T. aemula* are plain blue, the column white, flushed pale purple with a narrow (usually purple) band near the top. The midlobe is not hooded, the upper margins bright yellow and irregularly toothed. Intermediate lobes are less prominent than on *T.* aff. *ixioides*. The column-arms bear thin tufts of white hairs. It flowers in November and December.

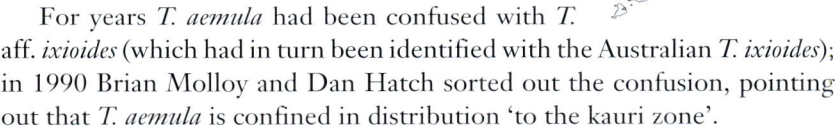

For years *T. aemula* had been confused with *T.* aff. *ixioides* (which had in turn been identified with the Australian *T. ixioides*); in 1990 Brian Molloy and Dan Hatch sorted out the confusion, pointing out that *T. aemula* is confined in distribution 'to the kauri zone'.

Thelymitra carnea

The leaf of this small *Thelymitra* is almost cylindrical, and grooved in front. The stem is a loose zigzag. The flowers are few, and may be cream through yellow to pink. The column is pinkish with a darker band near the top, the midlobe slightly hooded and

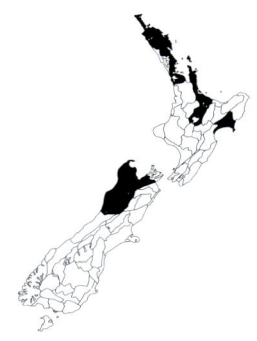

Thelymitra carnea. ES

bright yellow. The column-arms are oblique, bright yellow, with toothed upper margins and no cilia. It flowers from September to November.

Robert Brown described this taxon from Australia in 1810; Colenso and Sinclair sent yellow-flowered New Zealand specimens to Hooker who declared it different, and called it *T. imberbis* (unbearded, to signify the lack of cilia). Later authors found it to be identical with the Australian *T. carnea*, but now again there appears to be doubt, so the plant may be *T. imberbis* Hook.f. after all.

Thelymitra circumsepta

A tall, very robust plant of 50 cm or so, with a wide, thick and heavy leaf more or less erect, sheathing the stem for perhaps half its height. It has up to 18 flowers, each 1.5 cm across, rarely opening; the petals and sepals are all similarly shaped, blue, yellow-tipped, and lacking stripes or spots. The column-arms are flattened, emerge from the inner surfaces of the sides of the column, and bear rather coarse yellow hairs from their edges; a third column-arm, sometimes also bearing hairs, often rises centrally in front of the stigma. The midlobe is bright red and thickened into long calli. There are side-lobules, taller than the anther, with toothed margins.

T. circumsepta is uncommon, it flowers in December, and is clearly predominantly self-pollinating.

Colenso found what he called *T. formosa* in 1882, 'In clayey ground, *Fagus* woods, high land between Norsewood and Dannevirke, Waipawa County; flowering in December.' The plant is now regarded as identical with the Australian *T. circumsepta*, described and illustrated by Robert Desmond FitzGerald in 1878. FitzGerald wrote, 'This species is, I believe, wholly self-fertilized, and the third wing in front of the stigma seems to render hybridization by the visits of insects improbable.'

Thelymitra cyanea

T. cyanea has a thin leaf, thickened at the edges and midrib to make a trefoil shape in cross-section. The flower is 1–1.5 cm long, usually dark blue,

Thelymitra circumsepta. RT

Thelymitra cyanea. ES

occasionally pink or white, with thick, darker stripes on the petals and sometimes the sepals. The labellum is more clearly different from the other petals and sepals than in other thelymitras, larger, broader at the tip and more folded, and the lateral sepals may be quite narrow. The column-arms are flat, yellow, twisting in a short corkscrew without hairs, their tips sometimes notched. The column is purplish at the base, with broad blue vertical stripes. There is no midlobe, but clear calli lie behind the anther. The anther is almost fully exposed, and ends in short points.

• Chatham
• Auckland Is.

T. cyanea is common in swamps and bogs, montane subalpine in the north, but to sea-level in the south. It flowers from November to March; it is predominantly self-pollinating.

The first New Zealand description was by J.D. Hooker in the *Flora Antarctica* of 1844, of a specimen found in the Auckland Islands, and identified as as *T. uniflora*. Hooker was 'very uncertain as to the genus of this plant', and suspected that it was similar to the Australian species Lindley had called *Macdonaldia cyanea*. Afterwards the Robert Brown name of *T. venosa* was used for New Zealand plants, until the error was recently recognised, Hooker's suspicion confirmed, and the name *T. cyanea* applied.

Thelymitra x *dentata*

Recently shown to be a natural hybrid between *T. pauciflora* and *T. pulchella*. The flowers are pink to blue, heavily striped. The midlobe of the column is warty, dark red-brown with yellow margins; the column-arms have toothed margins and tufts of yellow-brown hairs.

Thelymitra hatchii

Another robust *Thelymitra* species, up to 40 cm tall, the leaf wide and strap-like. The flower is larger than most, 2 cm across, the blue-purple petals and sepals often yellow-edged and pointed, lacking stripes or spots. The column-arms are round in cross-section, and bear tufts of many pale yellow hairs, standing erect above the tall midlobe, which appears to be cut squarely across, red with a yellow edge, toothed and pointed. It grows mostly on dry clay banks, in gravel or under short scrub with plenty of light, and is fairly common. It flowers from November to January, and is predominantly self-pollinating.

Lucy Moore named this species in 1968 in honour of Dan Hatch, 'who reviewed and illustrated the orchids of New Zealand in a comprehensive series of papers from 1945 to 1952, and has since continued to grow and study these plants.'

Opposite: above, *Thelymitra* x *dentata*. R Lamberts; below, *Thelymitra hatchii*. IStG

Thelymitra intermedia

This taxon has been regarded as identical with small forms of *T. pauciflora*, a name which contains many forms. It is a predominantly reddish-stemmed plant, the leaf wide, channelled and fleshy, with red tints. The few flowers are slender, blue to dusky pink with no stripes or spots, a centimetre or so in diameter, the similarly shaped petals and sepals barely opening. The column-arms are round in cross-section, more or less erect, bearing rather sparse white hairs. The apex of the column midlobe is not thin and turned under as in *T. pauciflora*, but almost as in *T. longifolia* though more deeply cleft. The midlobe is dark with yellow edges. *T. intermedia* flowers early — October to November. Common except in the far south, it is predominantly self-pollinating.

The Swede Sven Berggren found *T. intermedia* in 1875, and the identity of his plant has been a source of controversy ever since.

Thelymitra intermedia. IStG

Thelymitra aff. *ixioides*. IStG

Thelymitra aff. *ixioides*

This New Zealand taxon differs from the Australian *T. ixioides* in that the New Zealand plant is self-pollinating while the Australian is insect-pollinated. The flowers are pink or blue, the petals spotted or occasionally plain. The column is pale blue, with a transverse violet band near the top, the midlobe not hooded, the upper margin bright yellow or red and studded with tall calli. The side-lobules are distinctly higher. The column-arms bear thin tufts of white or mauve hairs. It flowers from October to December.

Thelymitra longifolia

The common sun orchid, *T. longifolia*, grows on clay banks and in grassland, and under scrub. The leaf is wide, strap-shaped and long, not as stiff as that of many thelymitras, and lies along the ground. The plant can be quite variable in shape and size, the flowers white or tinged pinkish, grey-green backed. Up to 20 buds may form; the flowers can be 1.5 cm across, lacking spots or stripes. The column-arms are round in cross-section, bent forward, each carrying a cottonwool tuft of white hairs lying under the midlobe, which is dark brown and smooth, with a yellow semicircular unnotched or shallowly notched margin.

T. longifolia can be pollinated by insects, but can also self-pollinate. This means that in a dry season one may see the flowers open to the sun, but in a wet summer the flowers may never open. I have watched plants week after week, waiting for the flowers, only to find that fruit had formed under the buds without a flower ever having appeared. It is common, and flowers from November to January.

J.R. Forster noted in his diary in November 1773, after an outing to Long Island, Queen Charlotte Sound: 'We returned to dinner, having found . . . another new plant nearly relating to the class of Orches, but of a very singular structure & making absolutely a new genus.' The plant had been found by Banks and Solander during Cook's first voyage, and called 'Serapias regularis'. The Forsters named it *Thelymitra*.

Thelymitra longifolia. IStG   Opposite: *Thelymitra* aff *longifolia*. IStG

Thelymitra aff. *longifolia*. This is the tag-name given to what are probably several undescribed taxa that appear to be insect-pollinated. A range of plants with structural similarities to *T. longifolia* uncharacteristically exhibit the signs of insect pollination: they are scented, and all the large white to dark pink flowers on a stem open at once; solitary native bees have been seen to remove pollinia.

Thelymitra malvina

An orchid identified as the Australian species *T. malvina* is found only in the Far North, its flowers mauve or blue, its sepals and petals large and narrow. The midlobe of the column is hooded and narrow, scoop-shaped, purplish brown, its apex yellow. The column-arms bear tufts of mauve hairs.

T. malvina flowers from September to October. At Lake Ohia it may grow directly from rotting 30,000-year-old kauri stumps.

Thelymitra malvina. IStG

Thelymitra matthewsii. ES

Thelymitra matthewsii

An occasional trans-Tasman vagrant, rediscovered in the Far North in recent years, and still very hard to find there, though as the area is more carefully searched, greater numbers are being found. It seems to like bare broken clay or sandy areas where there is little competition from other plants. The leaf is expanded at the base, then narrows abruptly to form a helix around the stem. The one or two flowers are purple with darker stripes, the column purple at the base merging into yellow at the top, with no midlobe. The column-arms are bright yellow, oblong-curved, blunt, and without hairs. The large yellow anther-cap takes the place of the usual *Thelymitra* midlobe. It flowers August–September.

Thelymitra media

A trans-Tasman species which, it was recently revealed, grows in New Zealand and has been confused with *T. aemula*.

Thelymitra nervosa

This is a dark lavender-blue or pink, unstriped species, the petals sometimes (though not always) spotted, the column blue with thick erect white hairs on the horizontal arms, and a dark brown slightly hooded midlobe that is warty with dark tubercles and a yellow-toothed rim. It grows to 30 cm and has up to 6 flowers of 1.5 cm diameter. The hairs on the column-arms extend above the midlobe. The leaf is thin, channelled and keeled. *T. nervosa* is found on dry clay banks under manuka; it flowers from October to January, and is predominantly self-pollinating.

Cheeseman described *T. decora* from near Taupo in the appendix to his *Manual* of 1906, but Colenso had previously described *T. nervosa*, and the two are now regarded as identical.

Thelymitra nervosa. ES

Thelymitra pauciflora. YC

Thelymitra pauciflora

The plants we have identified with the Australian *T. pauciflora* are robust orchids, though variable in size and flower shape and colour. The flowers are usually mauve, shading to magenta, often strikingly beautiful, and lack spots or stripes. There are up to 10 on a stem, the petals and sepals pointed and long, the flower 3 cm across. The column is pale blue, its midlobe blackish purple, deeply cleft, the tapered margins bright yellow and incurved. The column-arms bear short, erect tufts of white, occasionally mauve, hairs. It flowers from November to January.

Lucy Moore noted the difficulty in naming the plant, and wrote:

> The name *pauciflora* is used here [*Flora of New Zealand*, Volume II] for plants in which the two sides of the narrow cleft are smoothly incurved so that their margins are usually not visible; correlated characters seem to be exceptionally stiff white cilia, early flowering, the flowers apparently able to set seed without the perianth having opened, and marked general reddish colouring of the whole plant in exposed places.

Currently there seems to be doubt that true *T. pauciflora* is in New Zealand at all.

Thelymitra pulchella

Another rather variable orchid, which may be a complex of several taxa. *T. pulchella* ('beautiful') is easily found; there are usually clumps of several plants

Thelymitra pulchella. ES

together, their flowers bright stars in open grassland. It is a thick-stemmed, robust plant with a wide, keeled leaf. There are up to half a dozen flowers on the stem, a few open at a time, and each 1.5 cm across, blue or pink (sometimes white), decorated with darker stripes on the petals and sepals. The column-arms are flat and reddish, bearing coarse seaweed-like red-orange-yellow fringes. The midlobe is variable, sometimes thickened, tuberculate, reddish and edged with yellow. It is common, especially in the south, and flowers from November to January; it is predominantly self-pollinating.

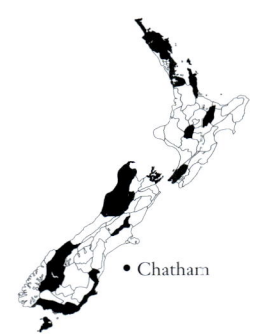

Thelymitra sanscilia

Moore regarded this as an aberrant form of *T. pauciflora*; others now regard it as a distinct species. It is generally similar to *T. pauciflora*, but the column-arms have few or no hairs, and the midlobe is often very deeply cleft and sometimes greenish. Found only in Northland, it flowers in October.

Thelymitra sanscilia. IStG

Thelymitra tholiformis. ES

Thelymitra tholiformis

The column is often similar in colour to *T. aemula*, but it lacks the intermediate lobes of that species. The yellow margins of the midlobe arch inwards and almost meet to form a dome. It flowers from November to December.

Thelymitra 'Ahipara'

A self-pollinating taxon so far found only in the Far North; it resembles *T. intermedia* when open, but the flowers never open in the wild, so the plant even in full mature flower appears to be in bud. It grows in peatbog pools, flowers in November and has flattened bright green leaves.

Thelymitra 'Comet'

This is the tag-name for a large, late-flowering taxon which is probably a sterile natural hybrid. It was found in the Kaweka Ranges where it is local and rare, where the clear mauve flower opens freely even on dull days. The

Thelymitra 'Ahipara'. GC

Thelymitra 'Comet'. DM

Thelymitra 'darkie'. IStG   *Thelymitra* 'rough leaf'. IStG

Thelymitra 'Whakapapa'. ES

column is white with a yellow apex; the midlobe strongly brownish red; cilia white, coarse, straight and rather dense — quite unlike those of *T. longifolia*. The top of the column is very prominently hooded. It flowers in January and seems not to set seed.

Thelymitra 'darkie'

An upright plant, all its parts including the stem are dark purple pigmented. Otherwise it is rather similar to *T. pauciflora*, although the apex of the column is blunt, not tapered or inrolled. It flowers in September.

Thelymitra 'rough leaf'

A robust plant, outwardly similar to *T. pauciflora* except that the pink flowers have 'chunkier', more rounded sepals and tepals, and the back of the upright leaf is rough to the touch. As in *T.* 'darkie' and *T. intermedia* the column apex is blunt. It flowers in October, though the flowers only rarely open. It is found only in Northland.

Thelymitra 'Whakapapa'

This taxon resembles a small, mauve-pink *T. longifolia*, but mature plants have short, narrow, more or less upright leaves. Triangular spurs (not always well-developed) high on the column-wings give them an unusual rectangular appearance. It flowers late, in January, and is known only from Ruapehu and Taranaki.

TOWNSONIA

A genus of 2 species, until 1998 regarded as identical and sometimes included in *Acianthus*. The Tasmanian species is *T. viridis*.

Townsonia deflexa. ES

Townsonia deflexa

This is a slender, erect ground orchid up to 10 cm tall, with a green oval 1 cm leaf halfway up the stem, and another leaf sometimes found at the base of the plant or at some distance from it.

The flowers are 5 mm long, 2–4 on a stem, horizontal and greenish. The dorsal sepal and labellum are broad, the other sepals long and keeled, the petals short and upright. The creeping rhizome is fleshy and bears small tubers.

Local small populations grow in dark mossy upland beech-forest floors. It is rare in the North Island, more common in the South; it also grows on Stewart Island and Auckland Island. It flowers in early December, and is predominantly self-pollinating.

William Townson wrote in 1906, 'I had the good fortune to discover in the same situation [Mount Rochfort] a little orchis which forms a new genus, and which Mr Cheeseman has honoured me by naming *Townsonia*.' T.F. Cheeseman wrote in his *Manual of the New Zealand Flora*: 'A very curious little plant . . . Believing it to be the type of a new genus, I have much pleasure in dedicating it to its discoverer, Mr. W. Townson, of Westport.'

Townsonia deflexa. ES

WAIREIA

Newly recognised as a monotypic genus in New Zealand, the plant was until recently regarded as a species of the Australian genus *Lyperanthus*.

Waireia stenopetala

This upright, stiff, 10 cm high plant has a pair of long narrow leaves hugging a stem that bears 2 or 3 flowers. These are 1–2 cm long, yellow green with brown blotches on a cap-like dorsal sepal which arches over and hides the rest of the flower. Often a vestigial bud is found beneath the top flower.

The species favours alpine scrub and herbfields — a wet, peaty, mossy habitat in high, cold places, where it is common enough in the south, but hard to find in the north. It becomes even rarer as the swamps are drained. Flowering is from December to February. The species is predominantly self-pollinating.

J.D. Hooker found what he took to be a *Thelymitra* in the Auckland Islands; he wrote in his *Flora Antarctica* of 1844: 'I have closely compared my very indifferent specimens of this plant with the several species of New Zealand and Tasmania and have no hesitation in describing it as new.' He called it *Thelymitra stenopetala*. He found another plant there, but at first could not identify it, and wrote: 'The plant has some points in common with *Chiloglottis* R.Br., but the leaves are not like those of that genus.' He decided what he thought it was during the printing of the work, however, and wrote in the Appendix, '*Lyperanthus antarcticus* . . . Though somewhat different in habit from the New Holland species, I do not think that this can be generically separated from them.' Clements, Jones and Molloy discovered that both specimens were of the same taxon, and renamed it *W. stenopetala* in 1998.

Opposite: *Waireia stenopetala*. IStG

WINIKA

New Zealand was thought until now to have one of the thousand or so southern Asian and Pacific dendrobiums, but this plant has recently been reassigned to a new monotypic endemic genus, *Winika*. The authors explain the new name:

Winika cunninghamii. ES

Winika is the accepted old Maori name for this orchid. The name Te Winika was given to the sacred war canoe of the Tainui people because this orchid grew on the totara tree (*Podocarpus totara*) which was hollowed out to form the hull (Moore & Irwin, 1978). We assign the feminine gender to it — *Winika cunninghamii*. The Maori Queen, Te Arikinui Dame Te Atairangikaahu, has granted consent for us to use the name Winika, because of its particular cultural significance to her Tainui people.

Winika cunninghamii

W. cunninghamii, which has the most beautiful of our orchid flowers, has been called lady's slipper because of the shape of the bud.

The 3 cm flower has white to green petals and sepals with a 3-lobed labellum attached to the column by a column-foot, which secretes a droplet of nectar. The lateral lobes of the labellum are usually pink or purple, though an entirely white form is sometimes found. The stems are long, branching, yellow canes, the fine stems wiry and brittle, the leaves pointed, 3 cm long by 3 mm wide.

In a good summer there may be hundreds of flowers on plants of several metres in diameter. It grows throughout New Zealand, most abundantly in wet lowland forests, sometimes on tree trunks, or as clumps the size of small shrubs on horizontal upper tree limbs. It finds the same sort of well-lit habitats on rock outcrops or cliffs, or hard-rock shores of lakes such as Waikaremoana, Manapouri and Te Anau, growing with low shrubs outside the forest edge. At Stewart Island it drapes the coastal banks in sheltered bay heads, growing on forest edges of well-drained peaty soil.

It is fairly common, but has been overgathered near population centres. *W. cunninghamii* flowers from December through January, and is predominantly insect-pollinated.

A list of the New Zealand orchids

This list reflects a personal view, gleaned from reading, conversation and observation. The last 'official' taxonomic treatment of the New Zealand orchids was by Lucy Moore in Moore & Edgar's *Flora of New Zealand II* in 1970; the notes refer to changes since then.

Acianthus sinclairii JD Hook. *Flora Novae Zelandiae* 1:245 (1853): *Flora II* called it *Acianthus fornicatus* var. *sinclairii*.

Adenochilus gracilis JD Hook. *Flora Novae Zelandiae* 1:246 t56A (1853).

Aporostylis bifolia (JD Hook.) Rupp & Hatch *Proc. Linn. Soc. NSW.* 70:61 (1946).

Bulbophyllum pygmaeum (Smith) Lindl. *Gen. Spec. orch. Pl.* 58 (1830).

Bulbophyllum tuberculatum Col. *Trans. N.Z. Inst.* 16:336 (1884).

Caladenia alata R.Br. *Prodr.* 324 (1810): *Flora II* called it *C. carnea* as var. *exigua*. See Hatch E.D. and McCrae D., *N.Z.N.O.G. Newsletter.* 32:5–6 (1989).

Caladenia atradenia D.Jones et al. *Orchadian* 12 (5):221 (1997): *Flora II* called it *C. carnea* var. *minor* forma *calliniger*. Has been confused with the Australian *C. iridescens*, and was also called *C.* aff. *iridescens*.

Caladenia bartlettii D.Jones et al. *Orchadian* 12 (5):221 (1997): *Flora II* called it *C. carnea* var. *bartlettii*. It has been confused with *C. carnea*.

Caladenia aff. *carnea*: the common pink form found throughout New Zealand, once mistaken for *C. catenata* which is now regarded as an Australian endemic.

Caladenia chlorostyla D.Jones et al. *Orchadian* 12 (5):221 (1997): was tagged *C.* 'green column'. '*Caladenia viridis*' is a small green early-flowering *Caladenia* from the Far North, described in H.B. Matthews's unpublished manuscript.

Caladenia lyallii JD Hook. *Flora Novae Zelandiae.* 1:247 (1853); there may be two or three taxa currently included in *C. lyallii* agg. — see Gibbs M. *N.Z.N.O.G. Journal*; 35:19 (1990), The *New Zealand Orchids: Natural history and cultivation* t20, and St George. *N.Z.N.O.G. Journal* 63:4 (1997).

Caladenia minor JD Hook. *Flora Novae Zelandiae.* 1:247 t56b (1853): *Flora II* called it *C. carnea* var. *minor.*

Caladenia nothofageti D.Jones et al. *Orchadian* 12 (5):221 (1997).

Caleana minor R.Br. *Prodr.* 329 (1810): occasional trans-Tasman vagrant, not a *Paracaleana*.

Calochilus herbaceus Lindl. *Gen. Spec. orch. Pl.* 459 (1840): a trans-Tasman vagrant, in *Flora II* as *C. campestris*, has been identified as *C. herbaceus*, though there seems to be some doubt as to its identity. See McCrae D., *N.Z.N.O.G. Newsletter* 24:9. (1987).

Calochilus paludosus R.Br. *Prodr.* 320 (1810).

Calochilus robertsonii Benth. *Flora Austral.* 6:315 (1873).

Chiloglottis cornuta JD Hook. *Flora Antarct.* 1:69 (1844). A trans-Tasman species with broad variation currently under study.

Chiloglottis formicifera Fitzg. *Austral. Orch.* 1(3): t9 (1877): occasional trans-Tasman vagrant, not seen in New Zealand for 50 years.

Chiloglottis valida DL Jones. *Australian Orchid Research* 2:43–4, 154 (1991): trans-Tasman vagrant, not in *Flora II*; has been mistaken for *C. gunnii*.

Corybas acuminatus Clements & Hatch. *N.Z.*

J. Bot. 23(3):491 (1985): *Flora II* mistakenly called it *C. rivularis* — q.v.).

Corybas carsei (Cheesem.) Hatch. *T.R.S.N.Z.* 75:367 (1945): *Flora II* included it in *C. unguiculatus*. See Irwin J.B., *N.Z.N.O.G. Newsletter* 23:8. (1987). May be identical to the Australian *C. fordhamii*.

Corybas cheesemanii JD Hook. Ex Kirk in *Trans. N.Z. Inst.* 3:180 (1871): *Flora II* included it in *C. aconitiflorus*. See Clarkson B.D., *Vegetation of Egmont National Park* (1986) p87.

Corybas cryptanthus Hatch. *T.R.S.N.Z.* 83:577 (1956).

Corybas dienemus DL Jones. *Flora of Australia*. 50:572 (1993): reported only from Macquarie Island; appears to be similar to *C. orbiculatus*.

Corybas iridescens Molloy & Irwin. *N.Z. J. Bot.* 34:1–10 (1996): was included by Irwin in the *C.* aff. *rivularis* group [q.v.] as *C.* 'A'.

Corybas macranthus (JD Hook.) HG Reichb. *Beitr. Syst. Pflk.* 67 (1871).

Corybas oblongus (JD Hook.) HG Reichb. *Beitr. Syst. Pflk.* 67 (1871): are there two forms? see Goodger R., *N.Z.N.O.G. Journal*. 61. (1996).

Corybas orbiculatus Col. *Trans. N.Z. Inst.* 23:389 (1891): this is not the taxon named *C. orbiculatus* in *Flora II*, but is that tag-named *C.* 'short tepals'; see Molloy B., *N.Z.N.O.G. Journal*. 51:12–14. (1994).

Corybas papa Molloy & Irwin. *N.Z. J. Bot.* 34:1–10 (1996): Irwin included it in the *C.* aff. *rivularis* group (q.v.) as *C.* 'Mt Messenger'.

Corybas rivularis (A.Cunn) HG Reichb. *Beitr. Syst. Pflk.* 67 (1871): this was Cunningham's original name and it is now applied to the plant Irwin tagged as *C.* 'Kerikeri' — see Molloy B.P.J. & Irwin J.B., *N.Z. J Bot.* 34:1–10 (1996). Irwin pointed out in 1989 that a range of taxa have affinities with *C. rivularis*; they were misnamed *C. orbiculatus* in *Flora II* and one is now known by the older Hatch name *C. macranthus* var. *longipetalus* as well as by Irwin's tag-name *C.* 'Waiouru'; others in the *C. rivularis* complex include *C.* 'Kaimai', *C.* 'rest area' and *C.* 'whiskers', [Irwin J.B. *N.Z.N.O.G. Newsletter* 32:1–4 (1989). *N.Z.N.O.G. Journal* 47:7–9 (1993). *N.Z.N.O.G. Journal* 55:22–24 (1995)]. See also *C. rivularis, C. orbiculatus, C. papa* and *C. iridescens*.

Corybas rotundifolius (JD Hook.) HG Reichb. *Beitr. Syst. Pflk.* 67 (1871): was included in *C. unguiculatus* and later tagged *C.* aff. *unguiculatus* — see Hatch E.D., *N.Z.N.O.G. Journal* 38:4–5. (1991).

Corybas trilobus (JD Hook.) HG Reichb. *Beitr. Syst. Pflk.* 67 (1871). A number of *Corybas* with trilobate leaves show differences in flowering time, size and sometimes structure [Gibbs M. *N.Z.N.O.G. Newsletter* 29:2–7 (1989)]. Variants in the *Corybas trilobus* complex include *C.* 'Trotters' [*N.Z.N.O.G. Newsletter* 28:10–13 (1988)], *C.* 'Rimutaka' [*N.Z.N.O.G. Journal* 58:8–9 (1996)], some possible *C. trilobus* hybrids with taxa having long dorsal sepals [ibid.; 58:4–7 (1996)], *C.* 'round leaf' and others.

Cryptostylis subulata (Labill.) HG Reichb. *Beitr. Syst. Pflk.* 15 (1871): trans-Tasman vagrant, now well established in Northland; not listed in *Flora II*. See Graham D.K.F., *N.Z. J. Bot.* 14:275. (1976).

Cyrtostylis oblonga JD Hook. *Flora Novae Zelandiae* 1:246 (1853): *Flora II* called it *Acianthus reniformis* var. *oblonga*. See Jones D. and Clements M., *Lindleyana* 2[3]:156. (1987).

Cyrtostylis reniformis R.Br. *Prodr.* 322 (1810): *Flora II* called it *Acianthus reniformis* var. *reniformis*. See Jones and Clements op. cit.

Danhatchia australis (Hatch) Garay & Christenson. *Orchadian* 11(10): 469–471 (1995): was known as *Yoania australis*.

Drymoanthus adversus (JD Hook.) Dockrill. *Australasian Sarcanthinae* 32:t3 (1967).

Drymoanthus flavus St George & Molloy. *N.Z. J. Bot.* 32:415–421 (1994).

Earina autumnalis (GJ Forst.) JD Hook. *Flora Novae Zelandiae* 1:239 (1853).

Earina mucronata Lindl. *Bot. Reg.* 20 (1814): includes the robust, late-flowering coastal form, '*E. aestivalis*'.

Gastrodia cunninghamii JD Hook. *Flora Novae Zelandiae* 1:251 (1853)

Gastrodia minor Petrie. *Trans. N.Z. Inst.* 25:273 t20 fig5–7 (1893).

Gastrodia aff. *sesamoides*: different from the Australian species *Gastrodia sesamoides* — see Ogle C., *N.Z.N.O.G. Journal* 51:9 (1994). There is variable tuberculateness of the flowers even among New Zealand plants.

Gastrodia 'long column' agg: there is clearly more than one undescribed *Gastrodia* with a long column. See Wilson H. *Field Guide — Stewart Island Plants* (1982) p294.

Genoplesium nudum (JD Hook.) D Jones & M Clements. *Lindleyana* 4(3):144 (1989): was included in *Prasophyllum* — see Hatch E.D., *N.Z.N.O.G. Newsletter* 37:18. (1991).

Genoplesium pumilum (JD Hook.) D Jones & M Clements. *Lindleyana* 4(3):144 (1989): was included in *Prasophyllum*— see Hatch E.D. *N.Z.N.O.G. Newsletter* 37:18. (1991).

Microtis arenaria Lindl. *Gen. Spec. orch.* Pl.306 (1840): see *N.Z.N.O.G. Journal* 58:16–18. (1996).

Microtis oligantha LB Moore. *N.Z. J. Bot.* 6: 473 fig.1 (1969).

Microtis parviflora R.Br. *Prodr.* 321 (1810): true *M. parviflora* may occur in New Zealand. See *N.Z.N.O.G. Journal.* 62.5–6. (1996). *Microtis* aff. *parviflora*: most New Zealand plants differ from *M. parviflora* in the strict sense: see *N.Z.N.O.G. Journal.* 62:5–6. (1996).

Microtis unifolia (JG Forst.) HG Reichb. *Beitr. Syst. Pflk.* 62 (1871). *M.* aff. *unifolia*: there may be more than one *Microtis* similar to true *M. unifolia*: see *N.Z.N.O.G. Journal.* 62:5–6 (1996) and. 67:4–6 (1998).

Orthoceras novae-zeelandiae (A.Rich.) M.Clements et al. *Australian orchid res.*; 1:100 (1989): was regarded as identical with the Australian *O. strictum*. But are both taxa in New Zealand? — see Goodger R., *N.Z.N.O.G. Journal*; 60. (1996).

Prasophyllum colensoi JD Hook. *Flora Novae Zelandiae.* 1:241 (1853).

Prasophyllum aff. *patens*: was regarded as identical with the Australian *P. patens*, but now regarded as an undescribed New Zealand taxon.

Pterostylis agathicola DL Jones et al. *Orchadian.* 12(6):266–281 (1997): was named *P. graminea* var. *rubricaulis* and later tag-named *P.* 'rubricaulis'.

Pterostylis alobula (Hatch) LB Moore. *N.Z.J. Bot.* 6:486 fig.3 (1969).

Pterostylis areolata Petrie. *Trans. N.Z. Inst.* 50:210 (1918).

Pterostylis australis JD Hook. *Flora Novae Zelandiae.* 1:248 (1853).

Pterostylis banksii A.Cunn. *Bot. Mag.* 59:t3172 (1832). *P. banksii* var. *silvicultrix* F. Muell. *Veg. Chath. Is.* 51 (1864) is a taxon from the Chatham Islands whose status is uncertain.

Pterostylis brumalis LB Moore. *N.Z. J. Bot.* 6:485 fig.3 (1969).

Pterostylis cardiostigma Cooper. *N.Z. J. Bot.* 21(1):97 (1983).

Pterostylis cernua DL Jones et al. *Orchadian* 12(6):266–281 (1997).

Pterostylis foliata JD Hook. *Flora Novae Zelandiae* 1:249 (1853).

Pterostylis graminea JD Hook. *Flora Novae*

Zelandiae 1:248 (1853).

Pterostylis humilis Rogers. *Trans. Roy. Soc. S. Aust.* 46:151 (1922).

Pterostylis irsoniana Hatch. *T.R.S.N.Z.* 78:104 pl.18 A–G (1950). *Pterostylis* 'haurangi' is a plant of uncertain status [affinities with *P. irsoniana*] from Haurangi State Forest Park; see *N.Z.N.O.G. Journal.* 67:3 (1998).

Pterostylis irwinii DL Jones et al. *Orchadian.* 12(6):266–281(1997): was tagged *P.* 'Erua'.

Pterostylis micromega JD Hook. *Flora Novae Zelandiae.* 1:248 (1853).

Pterostylis montana Hatch. *T.R.S.N.Z.* 77:239 pl.22 (1949). *Pterostylis* aff. *montana* agg: includes several undescribed taxa; for details of one of those currently tagged 'aff. *montana*', see *N.Z.N.O.G. Newsletter.* 25:12–14 (1988).

Pterostylis nutans R.Br. *Prodr.* 326 (1810): occasional trans-Tasman vagrant, recently rediscovered near Taupo — see *N.Z.N.O.G. Journal* 57:38–39 (1995).

Pterostylis aff. *obtusa:* plants found in 1998 near Nelson appear similar to Australian species in the *P. obtusa* group — see Donaghy et al. *N.Z.N.O.G. Journal* 68: 1998.

Pterostylis oliveri Petrie. *Trans. N.Z. Inst.* 26:270 (1893).

Pterostylis paludosa DL Jones et al. *Orchadian* 12(6):266–281 (1997): *Flora II* included it in *P. montana*, and it has been known as '*P.* linearis'.

Pterostylis patens Col. *Trans. N.Z. Inst.* 18:270 (1886): *Flora II* included it in *P. banksii*, but it is now regarded as distinct.

Pterostylis porrecta DL Jones et al. *Orchadian* 12(6):266–281 (1997): was *P.* aff. *graminea*.

Pterostylis puberula JD Hook. *Flora Novae Zelandiae.* 1:249 (1853): *Flora II* included it in *P. nana*, and it has been referred to as *P.* aff. *nana*.

Pterostylis tanypoda DL Jones et al. *Orchadian.*12(6):266–281 (1997): *Flora II* included it in *P. cycnocephala*, and it has been referred to as *P.* aff. *cycnocephala*.

Pterostylis tasmanica DL Jones. *Muelleria.* 8(2):177–192 (1994): *Flora II* included it in *P. barbata*; it has also been confused with *P. plumosa*. See Molloy B., *N.Z.N.O.G. Journal* 51: 14–16. (1994).

Pterostylis tristis Col. *Trans. N.Z. Inst.* 18:271 (1886): *Flora II* included it in *P. mutica*. See Molloy B., *Proc. 2nd Int. Orch. Conf.* 1985. p2.

Pterostylis trullifolia JD Hook. *Flora Novae Zelandiae.* 1:249 (1853).

Pterostylis venosa Col. *Trans. N.Z. Inst.* 28:610 (1896).

Pterostylis 'Catlins': undescribed; illustrated in St George. *Wild Orchids in the Far South of New Zealand* (1992).

Spiranthes sinensis (Pers.) Ames. *Orchidaceae.* 2:53 (1908).

Thelymitra aemula Cheesem. *Trans. N.Z. Inst.* 51:94 (1919): see Molloy B.P.J. and Hatch E.D., *N.Z.N.O.G. Journal.* 35:20–24. (1990). Jones (*Australian Orchid Research* Vol 3, 1998) says that *T. media* also occurs in New Zealand and has been confused with *T. aemula*.

Thelymitra carnea R.Br. *Prodr.* 314 (1810). Jones (*Australian Orchid Research* Vol 3, 1998) does not include New Zealand in the distribution of this species, hinting that our taxon may be different.

Thelymitra circumsepta FitzGerald *Australian Orchids* 1[4] (1878). Jones (*Australian Orchid Research* Vol 3, 1998) lists New Zealand in the distribution of this trans-Tasman species; it has been known here by the Colenso name *T. formosa*.

Thelymitra cyanea (Lindl.) Benth. *Flora Austral.* 6:323 (1873): *Flora II* included it in *T. venosa*. There appear to be two forms — see Beard C., *N.Z.N.O.G. Journal.* 59:29. (1996).

Thelymitra x *dentata:* a sterile hybrid of *T.*

longifolia and *T. pulchella:* see McCrae D.P. & Molloy B.P.J., *Ecosystems, Entomology & Plants.* RSNew Zealand Misc Series 48, 1998, p121.

Thelymitra hatchii LB Moore. *N.Z. J. Bot.* 6:477 fig.2 (1969).

Thelymitra intermedia Bergg. *Minneskr. Fisiogr. Sallsk. Lund Art.* 8,21,t5,f.21–24 (1878): regarded as identical with *T. pauciflora* [Molloy B.P.J. & Hatch E.D., *N.Z. J. Bot.* 28:105 (1990)], a name which however contains many forms — see below. Irwin and St George (*N.Z.N.O.G. Journal.* 58:25 (1996)] regard the plant tagged *T.* 'pseudopauciflora' as the rightful inheritor of this name).

Thelymitra aff. *ixioides*: differs from the Australian *T. ixioides*; the New Zealand taxon is self-pollinating, and the Australian species insect-pollinated.

Thelymitra longifolia JR et GJ Forst. *Char. Gen. Pl.* 98 t49 (1776). *Thelymitra* aff. *longifolia* agg: name given to some undescribed taxa that appear to be insect-pollinated.

Thelymitra malvina M.Clements et al. *Australian Orchid Research.* 1:141 (1989). Jones (*Australian Orchid Research* Vol 3, 1998) does not include New Zealand in the distribution of this species, hinting that our taxon may be different.

Thelymitra matthewsii Cheesem. *Trans. N.Z. Inst.* 43:177 (1911).

Thelymitra media R.Br. *Prodr.* (1810). See *T. aemula* above.

Thelymitra nervosa Col. *Trans. N.Z. Inst.* 20:207 (1888): *Flora II* called this plant *T. decora*; Morre was aware of Colenso's *T. nervosa* but could not place it at that time.

Thelymitra pauciflora R.Br. *Prodr.* 314 (1810). Jones (*Australian Orchid Research* Vol 3, 1998) does not include New Zealand in the distribution of this species, hinting that our taxa may be different.

Thelymitra pulchella JD Hook. *Flora Novae Zelandiae.* 1:244 (1853): there may be several plants with affinities to *T. pulchella* — the names *T. concinna* Colenso, *T. fimbriata* Colenso, *T. pachyphylla* Cheeseman and *T. caesia* Petrie have been treated as synonyms of *T. pulchella*, as Jones (*Australian Orchid Research* Vol 3, 1998) points out.

Thelymitra sanscilia Irwin ex Hatch. *T.R.S.N.Z.* 79:397 pl.81 (1952): Moore regarded this as an aberrant form of *T. pauciflora* — see *Flora II* p130 — others now regard it as distinct.

Thelymitra tholiformis Molloy & Hatch. *N.Z. J. Bot.* 28:105–114 (1990): identified as Berggren's *T. intermedia* by Moore, and included in *T. aemula* by Hatch: but see Molloy B.P.J. and Hatch E.D., *N.Z.N.O.G. Journal.* 35:20–24. (1990).

Thelymitra 'Ahipara': a cleistogamous, unnamed taxon.

Thelymitra 'comet': the tag-name for a large, late-flowering *Thelymitra* from the Kaweka range.

Thelymitra 'Whakapapa': undescribed — see *N.Z.N.O.G. Journal.* 54: 7–8. (1995).

Thelymitra 'darkie': undescribed.

Thelymitra 'rough leaf': undescribed.

Townsonia deflexa Cheeseman *Man. New Zealand Flora.* 692 (1906). *Townsonia viridis* is now regarded as a Tasmanian endemic (DL Jones: *Australian Orchid Research* Vol 3, AOF, 1998).

Waireia stenopetala DL Jones et al. *Orchadian.* 12(6):282–287 (1997): the species previously known as *Lyperanthus antarcticus*.

Winika cunninghamii MA Clements et al. *Orchadian.* 12(5):214–219 (1997): the species previously known as *Dendrobium cunninghamii*.

Table of flowering times

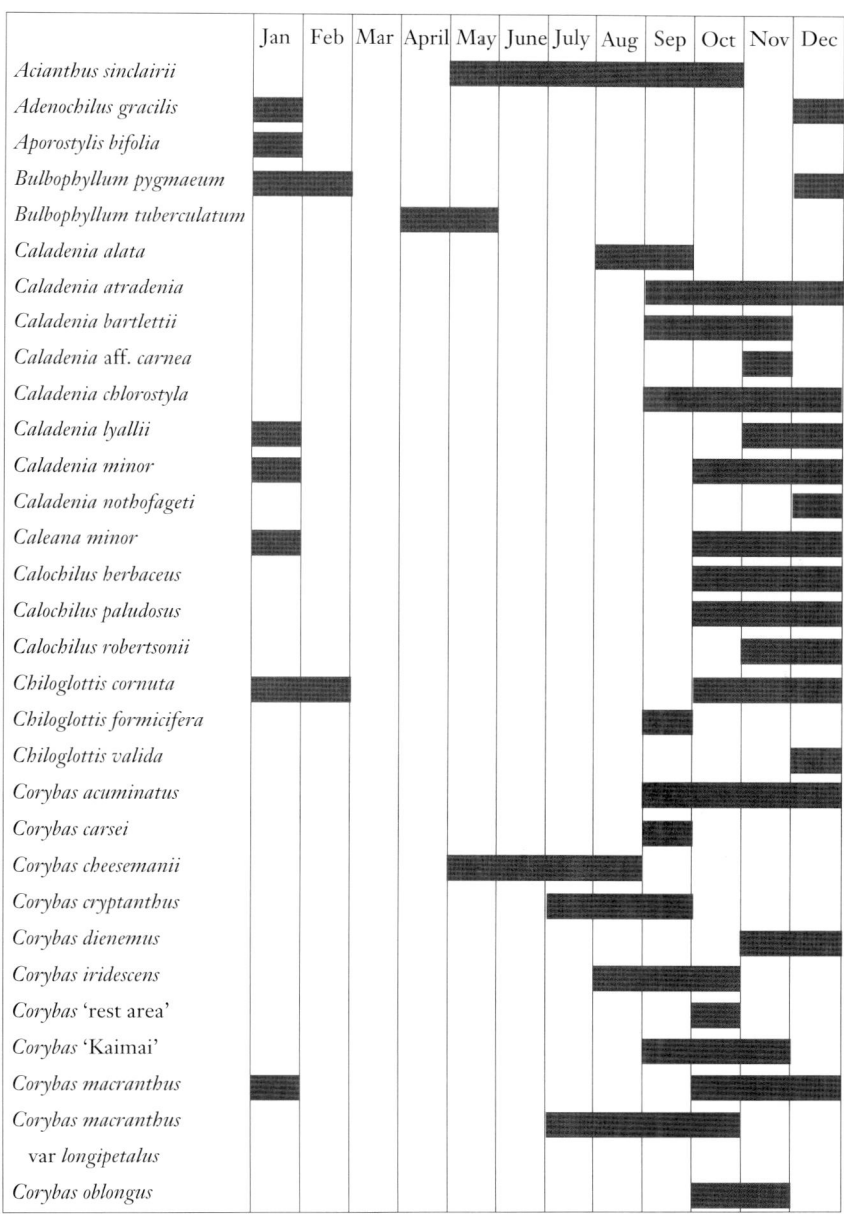

NEW ZEALAND NATIVE ORCHIDS 167

Species	Jan	Feb	Mar	April	May	June	July	Aug	Sep	Oct	Nov	Dec
Corybas orbiculatus								■	■			
Corybas papa								■	■			
Corybas 'Rimutaka'											■	
Corybas rivularis										■		
Corybas rotundifolius							■					
Corybas 'round leaf'										■	■	■
Corybas trilobus						■	■					
Corybas 'trotters'										■	■	■
Corybas 'whiskers'									■			
Cryptostylis subulata	■											■
Cyrtostylis oblonga												
Cyrtostylis reniformis							■	■	■			
Danhatchia australis	■											
Drymoanthus adversus										■	■	■
Drymoanthus flavus									■	■	■	
Earina autumnalis			■	■	■	■						
Earina mucronata	■								■	■	■	■
Gastrodia cunninghamii	■											
Gastrodia minor	■											
Gastrodia 'long column'	■											
Gastrodia aff. *sesamoides*										■		
Genoplesium nudum	■	■										
Genoplesium pumilum				■	■							
Microtis arenaria											■	
Microtis oligantha	■											■
Microtis parviflora	■	■										■
Microtis unifolia												
Orthoceras novae-zeelandiae	■	■										
Prasophyllum colensoi	■									■	■	■
Prasophyllum aff. *patens*												
Pterostylis agathicola							■	■	■			
Pterostylis alobula					■	■	■	■				
Pterostylis areolata									■	■		
Pterostylis australis										■	■	

168 NEW ZEALAND NATIVE ORCHIDS

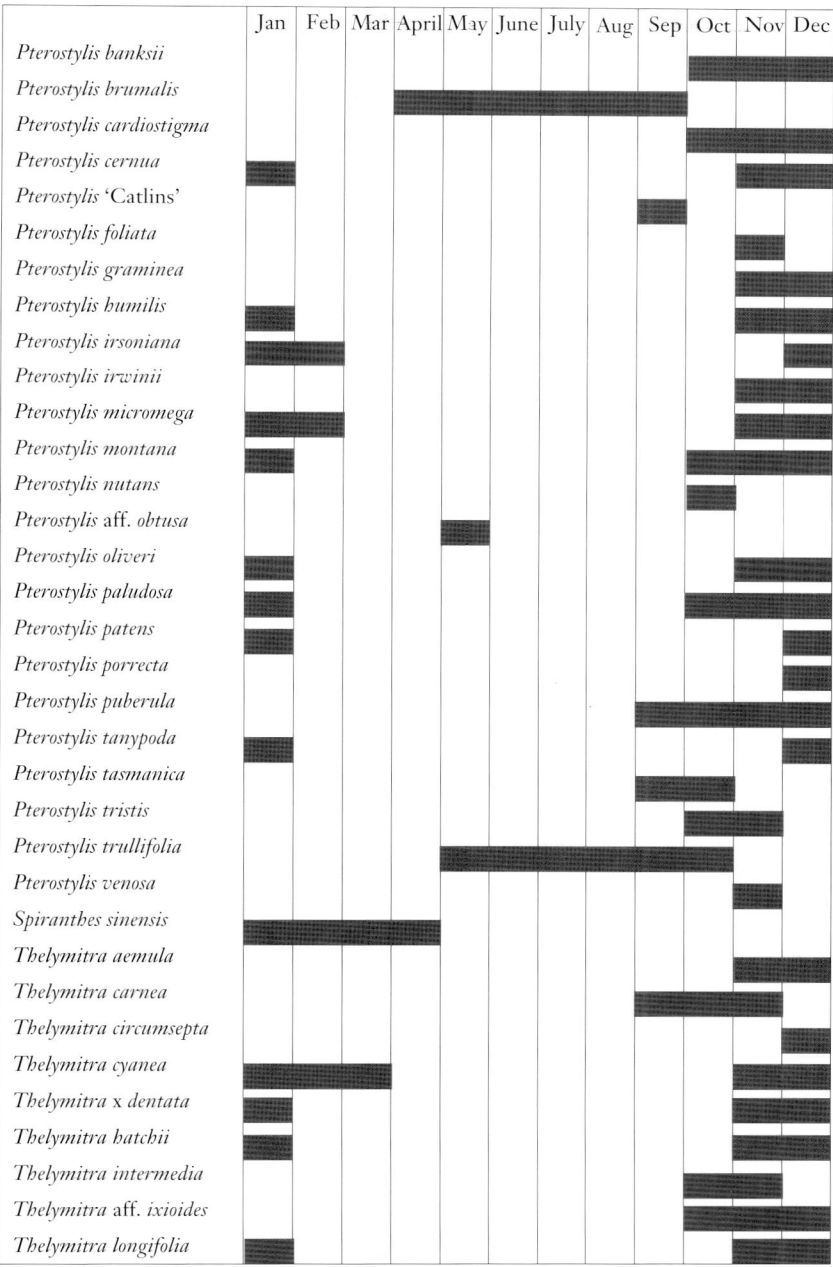

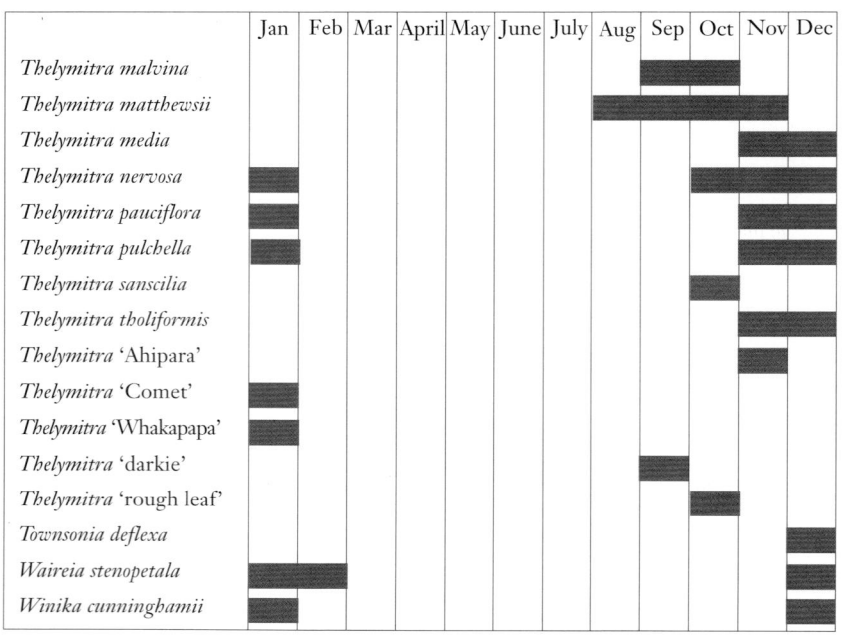

Derivations of specific names

acuminatus: the leaf tapering to a point
adversus: opposite (leaves)
aemula: emulating *ixioides*
agathicola: kauri (*Agathis*) dweller
alata: winged
alobula: without a little lobe
arenaria: growing in sandy areas
areolata: divided into small areas by the leaf veins
atradenia: dark glands
australis: southern
autumnalis: autumn (flowering)
banksii: named for Joseph Banks
bartlettii: named for Frank Bartlett
bifolia: 2-leaved
brumalis: winter (flowering)
cardiostigma: heart-shaped stigma
carnea: flesh (coloured)
carsei: named for Harry Carse
cernua: nodding
cheesemanii: named for Thomas Cheeseman
chlorostyla: green column
circumsepta: around the column (refers to the aberrant third staminode in the type specimen described by FitzGerald)
colensoi: named for William Colenso
cornuta: horn of plenty — the labellar calli
cunninghamii: named for Allan Cunningham
cryptanthus: hidden flower
cyanea: blue
dentata: toothed
dienemus: windswept
flavus: yellow (flowered)
foliata: leafy
formicifera: ant-bearing — the labellar calli
gracilis: slender
graminea: grasslike
hatchii: named for Dan Hatch
herbaceus: grassy
humilis: humble
intermedia: intermediate (between 2 other species)

iridescens: iridescent
irsoniana: named for Bruce Irwin and Owen Gibson
irwinii: named for Bruce Irwin
ixioides: like an Ixia
longifolia: long-leaved
lyallii: named for David Lyall
macranthus: large-flowered
malvina: mauve (cilia)
matthewsii: named for Richard Matthews
micromega: small (plant) large (flower)
minor: smaller
montana: montane
mucronata: the sharp-pointed leaves
nothofageti: of *Nothofagus* (beech) forest
nudum: naked — the absence of a leaf-lamina
nutans: nodding
oblongus: oblong — the leaf
oligantha: few-flowered
oliveri: named for Prof. Daniel Oliver of Kew
orbiculatus: round — the labellum — described from a dried specimen
paludosa (-us): swamp-growing
papa: found in papa clay soils
parviflora: small flowered
patens: open, expanded (sepals)
pauciflora: few-flowered
porrecta: stretched out and forward
puberula: downy
pumilum: very small
pygmaeum: very small
reniformis: kidney-shaped — the leaf
rivularis: (growing in) a stream
robertsonii: named for John Robertson
rotundifolius: round-leaved
sanscilia: lacking cilia
sesamoides: like sesamum
sinclairii: named for Andrew Sinclair
sinensis: Chinese
stenopetala: narrow petals
subulata: thin and pointed like an awl — the sepals
tanypoda: stretched-out stalk
tasmanica: of Tasmania
tholiformis: the dome-shaped midlobe of the column
trilobus: 3-lobed (leaves)
tristis: sad ('dingy-looking' wrote William Colenso)
trullifolia: trowel-leaved
tuberculatum: tuberculate, warty
unifolia: single-leaved
valida: strong growing
venosa: veined — the leaves — described from a dried specimen
viridis: green

Derivations of generic names

Acianthus: pointed flower
Adenochilus: gland-lip, referring to the massed calli on the labellum
Aporostylis: confusing column — this orchid was a taxonomic puzzle for many years
Bulbophyllum: bulb-leaf
Caladenia: lovely gland
Caleana: named for George Caley, an Australian orchidologist
Calochilus: lovely lip
Chiloglottis: lip-throat — is the labellum really like an Adam's apple?
Corybas: the corybantes were the dancing priests of Phrygia
Cryptostylis: hidden column (the flower is non-resupinate, its labellum uppermost)
Cyrtostylis: curved column
Danhatchia: named for Dan Hatch
Drymoanthus: forest flower
Earina: spring (flowering)
Gastrodia: stomach-shaped (the flowers are pot-bellied)
Genoplesium: having affinity with the genus *Prasophyllum*
Microtis: tiny ears (the column-wings)
Orthoceras: straight horn — the lateral sepals
Prasophyllum: leek leaf
Pterostylis: winged column
Spiranthes: spiral flowers
Thelymitra: woman's headgear (mitre)
Townsonia: named for William Townson
Waireia: from the Maori wai = water, rei = swampy ground
Winika: the Maori name for this orchid.

Reading list

The following contains useful material for those interested in studying the New Zealand orchids and their close relations. Much more has, of course, been recorded in the botanical literature: a full list of references would simply be too long, but recent work by Molloy and others, Jones and Clements has appeared in *The New Zealand Journal of Botany*, *The Orchadian* and *Muelleria*.

Arditti, J., *Fundamentals of Orchid Biology*, New York, Wiley, 1992.
Bates, R.J. & Weber, J.Z., *Orchids of South Australia*, Adelaide, Flora and Fauna of South Australia Handbooks Committee, 1990.
Bedford, R.B., *A Guide to Native Australian Orchids*, Sydney, Angus & Robertson, 1969.
Bishop, T., *Field Guide to the Orchids of New South Wales and Victoria*, Sydney, UNSW Press, 1996.
Black, J.M., *Flora of South Australia*, 3rd rev. ed., Jessop, J.P. (ed.), 1978.
Brown, R., *Prodromus Florae Novae Hollandiae et Insulae Van-Diemen*, London, J. Johnson et Sectos, 1810.
Cady, L. & Rotherham, E.R., *Australian Native Orchids*, Rev. 1985, Sydney, Reeds Books, 1970.
Chan, C.L. et al., *Orchids of Borneo. Vol 1*, Kota Kinabalu, Sabah Society, 1994.
Cheeseman, T.F., *Illustrations of the New Zealand Flora* (2 vols), Wellington, Government Printer, 1914.
— *Manual of the New Zealand Flora*, 1st ed., Wellington, Government Printer, 1906.
— *Manual of the New Zealand Flora*, 2nd ed., Wellington, Government Printer, 1925.
Clements, M.A., *Preliminary Checklist of Australian Orchidaceae*, Canberra, National Botanic Gardens, 1982.
— 'Australian Orchid Research' *Catalogue of the Australian Orchidaceae*, Essendon, Australian Orchid Foundation and Reed Books, 1989.
Comber, J.B., *Orchids of Java*, Kew, Royal Botanic Gardens, 1990.
Cooper, D.A., *A Field Guide to the New Zealand Native Orchids*, Wellington, Milburn & Co for the Wellington Orchid Society, 1981.
Costin, A.B. et al., *Kosciusko Alpine Flora*, Sydney, Collins, 1979.
Curtis, W.M., 'Pt 4A: Angiospermae: Orchidaceae', *The Student's Flora of Tasmania*, Hobart, Government Printer, 1979.
Dalrymple, H., *Orchid-hunting in Otago, New Zealand*, Dunedin, Coulls Somerville Wilkie, 1937.
Darwin, C., *The Various Contrivances by which Orchids are Fertilised by Insects*, 2nd ed., London, John Murray, 1904.
Dixon, K. et al., *Orchids of Western Australia*, 2nd ed., Victoria Park, West Australian Native Orchid Study and Conservation Group, 1989.
Dockrill, A.W., *Australasian Sarcanthinae; A Review of the Subtribe Sarcanthinae (Orchidaceae) in Australia and New Zealand*, Sydney, A.N.O.S., 1967.

— *Australian Indigenous Orchids*, Sydney, Society for Growing Australian Plants, 1969.
Dransfield, J. et al., 'Corybas West of Wallace's Line', HMSO *Kew Bulletin* offprint, London, 1986.
Ericson, R., *Orchids of West Australia*, Perth, Lamb, 1951.
Featon, E.H. and Featon, S.A., *The Art Album of New Zealand Flora, being a systematic and popular description of the native flowering plants of New Zealand and the adjacent islands*, Vol. 1, Wellington, Bock and Cousins, 1889.
FitzGerald, R.D., *Australian Orchids*, Sydney, 1879.
Forster, J.G.A., *Florulae Insularum Australium Prodromus*, Gottingen, Joann. Christian, Deiterich, 1786.
Forster, J.R. & Forster, J.G.A., *Characteres Generum Plantarum quas in Itinere ad Insulas Maris Australis Collegerunt, Descripserunt, Delinearunt*, London, White, Cadell & Emsly, 1776.
George, A.S., *Orchids of Western Australia*, Perth, Westviews, 1969.
Gibbs, M., *An Appreciation of the New Zealand Native Orchids of the Central Volcanic Plateau*, N.Z.N.O.G. Taupo Group and Taupo Orchid Society, 1989.
Gray, C.E., *Victorian Native Orchids*, Melbourne, Longmans, 1966.
Gray, M., & Burbridge, N.T. (illustrator), *Flora of the A.C.T.*, Canberra, Australian National University Press, 1970.
Halle, N., 'Orchidales', *Flore de la Nouvelle Caledonie et Dependences*, 8, Paris, Museum Nationale d'Histoire Naturelle, 1977.
Hatch, E.D., A series of papers in the *Transactions of the Royal Society of New Zealand 1945–1963*, 1945.
— *Auckland's Orchids*, Auckland Botanical Society, 1959.
Hoffman, N., & Brown, A., *Orchids of Southwest Australia*, Perth, University of Western Australia Press, 1992.
Holttum, R.E., 'Orchids of Malaya', Vol. 1 of *A Revised Flora of Malaya*, Singapore, Government Printing Office, 1953.
Hooker, J.D., *The Botany of the Antarctic Voyage. Flora Antarctica Part 1&2, Flora Novae Zelandiae, Flora Tasmanica*, London, Reeve, 1844–1860.
Hooker, J.D., *Handbook of the New Zealand Flora*, London, 1864.
Johns, J., & Molloy, B.P.J., *Native Orchids of New Zealand*, Wellington, Reed, 1983.
Johnson, M., *New Zealand Flowering Plants*, Christchurch, Caxton Press, 1968.
Jones, D.L., *Native Orchids of Australia*, Frenchs Forest, Reed Books, 1988.
— 'New Taxa of Australian Orchidaceae', *Australian Orchid Research*, 2, 62–65, 1991.
Laing, R.M. and Blackwell, E.W., *Plants of New Zealand*, 1st ed., Whitcombe and Tombs, 1906.
Lavarack, B., & Gray, B., *Australian Tropical Orchids*, Malanda, Frith & Frith, 1992.
Lewis, B.A. & Cribb, P.J., *Orchids of Vanuatu*, Kew, London, 1989.
— *Orchids of the Solomon Islands and Bougainville*, Kew, London, 1991.
Lothian, N., *Rosa Fiveash's Australian Orchids*, Adelaide, Rigby, 1974.
Mark, A.F., & Adams, N.M., *New Zealand Alpine Plants*, Auckland, Godwit, 1995.
Millar, A., *Orchids of Papua New Guinea*, Canberra, A.N.U. Press, 1978.
Moore, L.B. & Edgar, E., *Flora of New Zealand Volume II*, Wellington, Government Printer, 1970.

Moore, L.B., & Irwin, J.B., *Oxford Book of New Zealand Plants*, Wellington, Oxford University Press, 1978.
Natusch, S., *A Bunch of Wild Orchids*, Christchurch, Pegasus, 1968.
Nicholls, W.H., *Orchids of Australia Parts I–IV,* Melbourne, Georgian House, 1951.
Nicholls, W.H., *The Complete Edition—Orchids of Australia*, Melbourne, Thomas Nelson, 1969.
Pelloe, E.H., *West Australian Orchids*. Perth, Pelloe, 1930.
Anon., *Proceedings: 1st Australasian Native Orchid Conference and Show*, Sydney, Australasian Native Orchid Society, 1990.
— *Proceedings: 2nd Australasian Native Orchid Conference and Show*, Native Orchid Society of Toowoomba, 1993.
— *Proceedings: 3rd Australasian Native Orchid Conference and Show*, Adelaide, Native Orchid Society of South Australia, 1996.
Richard, A. & Lesson A.P., *Essai d'une Flore de la Nouvelle-Zelande*, Paris, 1832.
Rogers, R.S., *An Introduction to the Study of South Australian Orchids*, 2nd ed. rev. and enlarged, Adelaide, Government Printer, 1911.
Rupp, H.M.R., *Guide to the Orchids of New South Wales*, Sydney, Angus & Robertson, 1930.
— *The Orchids of New South Wales*, Sydney, National Herbarium (facs. ed. 1969), 1943.
Schlechter, R., *The Orchidaceae of German New Guinea*, English translation from the 1914 German ed. by Blaxell, DF., Melbourne, Australian Orchid Foundation, 1982.
Seidenfaden, G. & Wood, J.J., *The Orchids of Peninsular Malaysia and Singapore*, Fredensborg, Olsen & Olsen, pp 139–141, 1992.
Smith, J.J., *Die Orchideen von Java*, Leiden, Brill. Facs. ed. 1984, Delhi, Bishen Singh, 1908.
Société Néo-Calédonienne d'Orchido-phile, *Orchidées Indigènes de Nouvelle-Calédonie*, Nouméa, 1995.
Solander, D.C., *Primitiae Florae Novae Zelandiae sive Catalogus Plantarum in Eahei no Mauwe & Tavai Poenammoo*, Unpublished manuscript, 1769.
St George, I.M., *Wild Orchids in the Far South of New Zealand*, Dunedin, N.Z.N.O.G., 1992.
St George, I.M. & McCrae, D., *The New Zealand Orchids: Natural History and Cultivation*, Dunedin, N.Z.N.O.G., 1990.
Teo, C.H., *Native Orchids of Peninsular Malaysia*, Singapore, Times Books, 1985.
Thomson, G.M., *Introductory Class-book of Botany*, Wellington, Government Printer, 1891.
Van der Pijl, L. & Dodson, C.H., *Orchid Flowers; Their Pollination and Evolution*, Coral Gables, University of Miami Press, 1969.
Watson-Sharp, W., *Australia's Native Orchids*, Sydney, K.G. Murray Co, 1970.
Weber, J.Z. & Bates, R., 'Orchidaceae', in Jessop, J.P., & Toelkin, H.R., (eds), *Flora of South Australia*, Adelaide, S.A. Government Printing Division, 1986.
Wilson, H.D., *Field Guide— Stewart Island Plants*, Christchurch, Field Guide Publications, 1982.
Wood J.J., Beaman, R.S. & Beaman, J.H., *The Plants of Mount Kinabalu*, 2: Orchids, Kew, Royal Botanic Gardens, 1993.
Woolcock, C. & Woolcock, D., *Australian Terrestrial Orchids*, Melbourne, Thomas Nelson, 1984.

Index

Acianthus fornicatus 39
  rivularis 72
  sinclairii 38
Adenochilus gracilis 41
Aporostylis bifolia 42
Bulbophyllum pygmaeum 44
  tuberculatum 46
Caladenia alata 47
  alpina 53
  atradenia 48
  bartletti 49
  aff. carnea 50
  carnea var. barletti 49
  carnea var. minor forma calliniger 48
  catenata 50
  chlorostyla 50
  iridescens 48
  lyallii 52
  macrofilia 42
  minor 53
  nothofageti 54
  campestris 56
  herbaceus 56
  paludosus 58
  robertsonii 59
Chiloglottis cornuta 60
  formicifera 62
  valida 62
Corybas acuminatus 63
  carsei 64
  cheesemanii 65
  cryptanthus 66
  dienemus 67
  fordhamii 64
  iridescens 67
  'Kaimai' 74
  macranthus 69
  macranthus var. longipetalus 74
  oblongus 70
  orbiculatus 71
  papa 72
  'rest area' 74
  'Rimutaka' 78

  rivularis 72
  rotundifolius 76
  'round leaf' 78
  trilobus 77
  'trotters' 78
  unguiculatus 64, 76
  'whiskers' 74
Corysanthes matthewsii 76
  rotundifolia var. pandurata 72
Cryptostylis subulata 80
Cyrtostylis oblonga 81
  reniformis 81
Danhatchia australis 82
Dendrobium, see Winika
Drymoanthus adversus 85
  flavus 85
Earina aestivalis 91
  autumnalis 87
  mucronata 91
Gastrodia cunninghamii 93
  'long column' 95
  minor 94
  aff. sesamoides 97
Genoplesium nudum 98
  pumilum 99
Lyperanthus antarcticus 158
Macdonaldia cyanea 140
Microtis arenaria 100
  icrotis rara 102
  oblonga 102
  oligantha 100
  parviflora 102
  unifolia 102
Nematoceras rotundiflolia 76
Ophrys unifolia 103
Orthoceras novae-zeelandiae 104
Prasophyllum colensoi 105
  aff. patens 106
Pterostylia agathicola 109
  alobula 109
  aphylla 131
  areolata 110
  australis 110

Pterostylia banksii 113
   banksii var. *silvicultrix* 113
   barbata 130
   brumalis 114
   cardiostigma 115
   'Catlins' 122
   cernua 116
   cycnocephala 129
   foliata 116
   furcata 126
   graminea 117
   humilis 118
   irsoniana 118
   irwinii 120
   micromega 120
   montana 121
   mutica 129
   nana 128
   nutans 122
   aff. *obtusa* 124
   oliveri 124
   paludosa 126
   patens 127
   plumosa 130
   porrecta 128
   puberula 128
   tanypoda 129
   tasmanica 130
   tristis 131
   trullifolia 131
   venosa 131

Spiranthes sinensis 134
Thelymitra aemula 137
   'Ahipara' 152
   carnea 137
   circumsepta 138
   'comet' 152
   cyanea 138
   'darkie' 155
   decora 148
   x *dentata* 140
   formosa 138
   hatchii 140
   intermedia 142
   aff. *ixioides* 143
   longifolia 144
   malvina 146
   matthewsii 147
   media 147
   nervosa 148
   pauciflora 149
   pulchella 150
   'rough leaf' 155
   sanscilia 151
   stenopetala 158
   tholiformis 152
   'Whakapapa' 155
Townsonia deflexa 157
   viridis 156
Waireia stenopetala 158
Winika cunninghamii 161

Ian M St George MD FRACP FRNZCGP
John Street Doctors
27, Riddiford St, Wellington
Phone 04 3899039 Fax 3894178
istge @ rnzcgp.org.nz